The Grand Ole Opry

PRESENTS

THE YEAR IN COUNTRY MUSIC

The Grand Ole Opry

PRESENTS

THE YEAR IN COUNTRY MUSIC

GERRY WOOD

Villard Books
A Division of Random House, Inc.
A Byron Preiss/Janis A. Donnaud and Associates, Inc. Book

Library of Congress Cataloging-in-Publication data is available.
ISBN: 0-679-76308-2

A Byron Preiss/Janis A. Donnaud and Associates, Inc. Book

Book design by J. Gallardo

Printed in the United States of America on acid-free paper
2 4 6 8 9 7 5 3
First Edition

ACKNOWLEDGMENTS

First, thanks to my Opry friends: Bud Wendell, Bob Whittaker, Hal Durham, Jerry Strobel, Skeeter Davis, Jerry Clower, Bill Anderson, and Tom T. Hall.

Second, for support, encouragement, and inspiration: Reba McEntire and Narvel Blackstock, Jerry Jeff and Susan Walker, John and Robin Berry, Charlie Chase and Lorianne Crook, Charlie Monk, Mark Chesnutt, Ed Morris, Guy Clark, Vince Gill, Kathy Mattea, Tracy Byrd, the mystical Michael Martin Murphey, George Strait, Sam Phillips, Willie Nelson, Emmylou Harris, Steve Earle, Ty Herndon, Shannon Parks, Chrissy Coleman (who will be in these pages someday), Dolly Carlisle, Eileen Shannon, and the world's finest Harbor Master, Brandi Marquette. To Ellen Wood and Carol Shaughnessy, thanks for the long ride and the short haul.

To the greatest editor in all of Gotham City, Kathy Huck. Hopefully, she molded me into a Hillbilly Hemingway. Or at least into a Renaissance Redneck.

And, finally to those who have gone before the rest of us. God, I miss these guys: my folks, Gladys and Albert Wood, Bill Williams, Jack Stapp, Ed Shea, Ben Smathers, Keith Whitley, O. B. McClinton, Uncle Dick, Aunt Dora, and Cousin Shirley.

The work is dedicated to all of the above with love and respect forever.

Gerry Wood
Nashville, Tennessee
November 15, 1995

E N T S

The Grand Ole Opry

PRESENTS
THE YEAR IN COUNTRY MUSIC

1995

Alan Jackson certainly made 1995 his year, rounding up five trophies at the TNN/Music City News awards and winning CMA Entertainer of the Year.

THE WORLD'S GONE COUNTRY, LOOK AT THEM BOOTS

> He's gone country
> Look at them boots
> He's gone country
> Back to his roots. . . .
> —*From "Gone Country," sung by Alan Jackson
> and written by Bob McDill*

The year of the Lord 1995. Lord, what a year for country music! The global village became a down-home community as country music accelerated its growth as a dominant national—and, increasingly, international—art and entertainment form. Brilliant new artists, the new breed of multimillion-sellers, the solid contributions of the established superstars, and the renaissance of country's grizzled veterans have taken this music genre to new heights and to new frontiers with new promises.

1995—
•The year that Garth became a single name, like Elvis, and surpassed the King in record sales.
•The year that country caused a bull market in precious-metal stocks with its record lode of gold and platinum album sales.
•The year that country went from CD to CD-ROM.
•The year that country-music stars prevailed on TV, in videos, and in movies and as pitch persons for a variety of products, ranging from Fruit Of The Loom briefs to Visa credit cards.
•The year that the chords of country music resonated from Branson to Beijing. From Paris, Kentucky, to Paris, France. From Tennessee to Tokyo. From the Wild West to the Far East.
•The year that the Man in Black, Johnny Cash, wore white. Reba McEntire journeyed to the jungles of Guatemala to shoot a video. George and Tammy reunited on record and onstage. The Tractors plowed new ground all the way from Tulsa to Tennessee and beyond. And the Highwaymen—Johnny Cash, Waylon Jennings, Willie Nelson, and Kris Kristofferson—kept their vocal vehicle aimed straight down the blue highways of America.

Fan Fair was bigger and better than ever, and the Grand Ole Opry—celebrating its seventieth birthday—lived up to its Nashville billboards that proclaim WHO'LL SURPRISE US THIS WEEK? Festivals prospered across the country—Fanfest in California, WestFest in Colorado, and the Peach Festival in South Carolina.

Country music's family grew with babies—from new mom Martina McBride to happy dad Tracy Byrd—but, sadly, the world of country music lost such talents as Charlie Rich.

It was definitely the Year of the Dance, with line dancing, especially, becoming a national rage, spawning new dance clubs and dance crazes across the country.

And country music grew more presidential than ever, with a White House concert for President Bill Clinton and First Lady Hillary Rodham Clinton and two memorable Nashville visits by former president George Bush, who mingled with, and was honored by, his music-business friends.

But most of all, 1995 was the Year of Awards. Platinum was the metal of choice and gold a frequent second. Let's check the winner's circle:

COUNTRY MUSIC ASSOCIATION AWARDS

Alan and Alison were the big winners at the 29th Annual CMA Awards held on October 4, 1995. Alan Jackson walked off with the night's biggest prize—the Entertainer of the Year trophy—while Alison Krauss won four awards. The bluegrass star won the prestigious Horizon Award, Female Vocalist, and with her band Union Station, took Single of the Year honors for "When You Say Nothing at All." She topped off the memorable night by winning Vocal Event of the Year accolades for her duet with Shenandoah, another first-time winner.

Vince Gill, who hosted the CBS-TV telecast from the Grand Ole Opry House, won a record fifth consecutive Male Vocalist of the Year award. Patty Loveless accepted the Album of the Year trophy for *When Fallen Angels Fly*. Brooks & Dunn won their fourth straight Vocal Duo award. "Independence Day" by Gretchen Peters won Song of the Year.

The Mavericks climaxed their climb to the top by winning the award for Vocal Group of the Year. Another eclectic group, the Tractors, won for Music Video with their rollicking, daffy and delirious "Baby Likes to Rock It" video directed by Michael Salomon. Musician's musician Mark O'Connor, fiddler extraordinaire, was voted Musician of the Year.

Rounding out the evening, Roger Miller was inducted into the Country Music Hall of Fame. His widow Mary Miller told the audience, "Roger was a dreamer, and this would have been his wildest dream come true." Former CMA Executive Director Jo Walker-Meador, who

helped guide the CMA from its inception, was also inducted into the Hall of Fame.

ACM Awards

Reba McEntire became the first woman to win the Academy of Country Music's top award, Entertainer of the Year, since Barbara Mandrell won it back in 1980. Reba also won Top Female Vocalist at the glittery awards show televised from Los Angeles. Reba likes the idea of women at the top: "It's about time, and I'm glad they picked me," she told the media backstage. She revealed that, before being named as the winner, she was thinking, "I just keep working, wanting it, craving it, and maybe one day they'll feel sorry for me and give it to me."

Alan Jackson garnered the Top Male Vocalist trophy while John Michael Montgomery scored with two of the Academy's Hat Awards, Song of the Year and Single of the Year, for "I Swear."

Tim McGraw was honored as Top New Male Vocalist, then pulled a surprise by beating out Mary Chapin Carpenter, Vince Gill, Alan Jackson, and Garth Brooks for Album of the Year, with *Not a Moment Too Soon*. Another surprise was the Mavericks' coming of age—by winning the award for Top Vocal Group.

Brooks & Dunn accepted Top Vocal Duet honors while the beautiful newcomer Chely Wright gained the award for Top New Female Vocalist. Garth grabbed two honors—an award for Video of the Year for "The Red Strokes" and the prestigious Jim Reeves Memorial Award for helping to popularize country music overseas.

"What in the world is going on here, folks?" asks a stunned, but happy, Alison Krauss who won four CMA Awards.

The night's most emotional moment came as Loretta Lynn, who's had a tough year tending to her ailing husband, Mooney, won the Academy's Pioneer Award. She received a standing ovation from her country-music compatriots, including Reba, whose tears of joy washed away her makeup.

GRAMMY AWARDS

Mary Chapin Carpenter became the first country artist to win a Grammy Award four years straight in the same category. This time she won Best Country Performance, Female, for "Shut Up and Kiss Me." The National Academy of Recording Arts and Sciences honored Carpenter's brilliant collection of ballads, *Stones in the Road*, with Best Country Album.

TNN/MUSIC CITY NEWS AWARDS

Alan Jackson came out the big winner at the fan-voted TNN/Music City News Awards during Fan Fair Week. The lanky Georgian won five trophies—for Album (*Who I Am*), Song ("Livin' on Love"), Male Artist, Vocal Collaboration (a duet with his idol, George Jones—"A Good Year for the Roses"), and the night's top honor, Entertainer of the Year. His avalanche of awards prompted Reba McEntire, who won Female Artist of the Year honors, to feign mock shock that Alan didn't win her award, too. Jackson later joked, "Actually, I kind of wanted it." Look out next year, Reba.

Brooks & Dunn beat out the Statler Brothers, long-time TNN/Music City News Award recipients, for the Vocal Group or Duo of the Year award. And the hot-selling, quick-witted Jeff Foxworthy proved himself worthy of the Comedian of the Year trophy. Sawyer

With the video backdrop proclaiming his victory, Alan Jackson cheerfully accepts his Entertainer of the Year Award during the TNN/Music City Awards.

Brown was voted Top Vocal Band, Martina McBride's emotionally wrenching video of "Independence Day" justifiably claimed Best Video plaudits, and Ricky Van Shelton was chosen Favorite Christian Country Artist. Willie Nelson accepted the Minnie Pearl Award for his fund-raising Farm Aid concerts while his Texas buddy, Waylon Jennings, won the Living Legend Award. Looking toward the future of country music, the fans voted in three Star of Tomorrow categories, naming Faith Hill, Tim McGraw, and the group BlackHawk.

NASHVILLE MUSIC AWARDS

A new award show—the Nashville Music Awards (nicknamed the Nammies)—honored the tops in

Nashville talent, from country to bluegrass, gospel, soul, and rock. Winners included Chet Atkins (Instrumental Jazz Album), Amy Grant (Pop/Rock Album), Patty Loveless (Outstanding Country Album), Alison Krauss and the Cox Family (Bluegrass Album), Vince Gill (Male Vocalist), Trisha Yearwood (Female Vocalist), Rodney Crowell (Artist/Songwriter), the Mavericks (Group/Duo), and Mary Chapin Carpenter and Don Schlitz, whose "He Thinks He'll Keep Her" dominated as Best Song.

GOLDEN PICK AWARDS

Another new awards presentation allowed the fans to vote for their favorite artists: More than 135,000 mailed in ballots from every state in the country and every province in Canada as *Country Weekly* magazine staged its first Golden Pick Awards. TNN's *Music City Tonight* co-hosts Lorianne Crook and Charlie Chase presented the trophies at the ceremonies, which were held at the Grand Ole Opry House.

It was an awards-breakthrough night for Billy Ray Cyrus, who happily picked up three Golden Pick trophies for Star with the Biggest Heart (citing his humanitarian efforts), Favorite Line Dance ("Achy Breaky Heart"), and Dream Duet—readers wanted to see Billy Ray team up with Tanya Tucker. Often ignored at other awards shows, he told the audience, "I've had an achy breaky heart for a long time but this is going to help mend it a bit."

Confederate Railroad chugged to the Favorite Group ranking, John Anderson rebounded to the stage as Comeback Artist of the Year, and Loretta Lynn won a Lifetime Achievement Award. Favorite All-Time Male Vocalist was Johnny Cash, and David Ball accepted the award for Favorite

Male Newcomer, noting it was his first such honor. "I want to thank my relatives back in South Carolina for stuffing the ballot box," the quick-witted Ball quipped.

Some offbeat honors spiced up the night—Lorrie Morgan (Dream Date, Female), John Michael Montgomery (Dream Date, Male), Dolly Parton (Favorite for Hall of Fame Induction), and Tanya Tucker (Tomorrow's Legend). Legendary guitarist Chet Atkins was named Favorite Instrumentalist and put tongue firmly in cheek as he deadpanned, "I was hoping to get the newcomer award."

COUNTRY DANCE MUSIC AWARDS

Country's line-dancing craze has led to its own awards show—the Country Dance Music Awards, held at the Wildhorse Saloon in Nashville. Tracy Byrd's "Watermelon Crawl" proved to be a top dance favorite by winning both Favorite New Country Dance Step Choreography and Favorite Extended Country Dance Mix awards. The Tractors' "Baby Likes to Rock It" won Favorite Country Dance Song. Tim McGraw won the award for Favorite Dance Album with *Not a Moment Too Soon*.

CANADIAN COUNTRY MUSIC AWARDS

Michelle Wright won Entertainer of the Year, but Shania Twain won just about everything else during the 1995 Canadian Country Music Awards. Michelle also hosted the show that was televised from Hamilton, Ontario, by CTV and TNN: The Nashville Network.

Nominated in five categories, Shania swept all five—Female Vocalist, Album for *The Woman in Me*, Song for "Whose Bed Have Your Boots Been Under?" and Single and Video of the Year for "Any Man of Mine." Male

Vocalist winner was Charlie Major, Vocal Duo/Group was Prairie Oyster, Jim Witter and Cassandra Vasik won for Vocal Collaboration, while Farmer's Daughter received the Vista Rising Star award.

Radiating her talent and beauty like the winner she is, Shania Twain accepts one of her five trophies at the 1995 Canadian Country Music Awards.

Yes, 1995 proved that not only the nation but the world has gone country. They're line dancing in Ireland. Look at them boots in London. Country music and sushi bridge culture gaps in Japan. And it's starting to go on top down under in Australia. The explosion of this dynamic yet down-home music style has just begun. Let's see how it's pervading the lifestyle of America and cultures far beyond our borders.

Can't get enough? Here are more awards honoring country's top artists in 1995

AMA AWARDS
Reba McEntire—Favorite Female
Reba McEntire—Favorite Country Album, *Read My Mind*
Alabama—Top Group
Garth Brooks—Favorite Male Artist
Tim McGraw—Favorite New Artist
Vince Gill—Favorite Country Single for "Whenever You Come Around"

GREAT BRITAIN COUNTRY MUSIC AWARDS
Garth Brooks—International Male Vocalist
Garth Brooks—Touring Act
Garth Brooks—International Album
Mary Chapin Carpenter—International Female Vocalist
Brooks & Dunn—International Group/Duo
Martina McBride—International Video for "Independence Day"
Alan Jackson and Jim McBride—International Composer
for "Chattahoochee"
Charley Pride—Special Achievement Award
for lifetime international popularity

BROADCAST MUSIC INC. (BMI) AWARDS
Writers Tom Shapiro and Bob DiPiero—Robert J. Burton Award for the
Most Performed Country Song of the Year for "Wink" (performed by
Neal McCoy)
Vince Gill—Songwriter of the Year

AMERICAN SOCIETY OF COMPOSERS, AUTHORS, AND PUBLISHERS (ASCAP) AWARDS
Gary Baker and Frank Myers—Country Song of the Year for "I Swear"
(performed by John Michael Montgomery)
Gary Burr—Songwriter of the Year
George Strait—Voice of Music Award

SESAC AWARDS
Frank Dycus—Country Songwriter of the Year

With songs like the Tractors' "Baby Likes to Rock It," who could resist the new craze of country line-dancing?

COUNTRY

2

FROM FIELD AND STREAM
TO MAINSTREAM

Along with jazz and blues, and later rock and roll, country music became one of the few original art forms of
America just as classical, opera, and polka became trade-
mark musical gifts of Europe. Emigrants from such
homelands as Germany, Ireland, and England brought
their music with them when they crossed the seas to
North America in search of a better life. The tired, the
huddled, the poor were rich in heritage, blessed in

CULTURE

ballads, and masters at remembering the melodies that their ancestors handed down for generations.

The music took root like kudzu in red Georgia soil, in Appalachia, and in deep pockets of Texas. It came from the mountain folks down by the crystal-clear, cold streams and from the Plains pioneers, who forged their way westward toward their fields of dreams. Country music gained dimensions and depth, as America's melting pot added a dash of Cajun (via Louisiana, via Canada, via France), blues (whites and blacks of the South sang about the same worries and woes, only to different rhythms), and gospel (most country songs are basically about how to live, or how not to live, and what will happen if one chooses not to abide by the Golden Rule).

Let's fast-forward to 1995. The world has given to country music—its rhythms, rhymes, and reasons—and in 1995, country music gave back to the world—in spades. It crossed the oceans as never before, impacting on the cultures and mores of the places from which it came. Ingrained in the fabric of America, it now lends itself to the lifestyles of countries far beyond the borders of the United States. Playing off the momentum of country's global expansion in 1994, the international penetration of country music saw the genre reach new markets with a new audience.

In 1994, Garth Brooks sold 72,000 tickets in five hours to his shows in Dublin, Ireland. He returned to Ireland with his family in 1995 for a working vacation. Brooks, who has sold more than 500,000 albums in this country of 3.5 million, received an award from the Irish Recorded Music Association. He further won the hearts of the Irish by helping to raise money for the Irish Society for the Prevention of Cruelty to Children and for his reply to Pat

Kenny on the *Kenny Live* TV show, who asked why Garth had returned to Ireland: "Since becoming a star, many people treat us like royalty, but you take it one step further. You treat us like family."

"Nashville Comes to Ireland" brought country-music

singers, songwriters, and executives to Ireland for a Country Music Association board meeting as well as parties and performances. The country visitors met the Irish prime minister,

Clint Black poses outside his Dublin hotel during "Nashville Comes to Ireland."

John Bruton, and the U.S. ambassador to Ireland, Jean Kennedy Smith, who professed herself to be a country-music fan. Among those taking part in the four-day event were Kris Kristofferson, Clint Black, John Berry, and Marty Stuart, who explained the strong bond between Ireland and American country music. "Most of our fiddle tunes—and our ancestors—come from this part of the world," Marty noted. "It's only fitting, now that country music is moving onto the world stage, to come back to its homeland through the front door of Ireland."

Walking through that door onto the world stage this year was a record-breaking number of country artists. Kathy Mattea toured Scotland and England. Waylon Jennings wandered about on a ten-day media tour of the continent, plugging his album *Waymore's Blues (Part II)*. Europe also welcomed Trisha Yearwood, Emmylou Harris, Guy Clark, and Mary Chapin Carpenter. George Jones and Tammy Wynette took the reunion of the decade across the Atlantic to Ireland, England, and Switzerland. Don Williams went down under to Australia at the same time that the Cactus Brothers went to Estonia as the first country act to perform in that former Soviet republic.

Even video productions—in earlier years, low-budget close-to-home ventures—moved beyond the borders of the United States. Tim McGraw went to Mexico for a shoot, Reba McEntire journeyed to a remote mountain-top in Guatemala, and Shania Twain won the most fre-quent-flyer points with her video adventure set against the pyramids of Egypt.

C&W—does it stand for China & western? The coun-try thrust isn't ignoring China's vast population. China USA Entertainment Corporation is working to program western music through China National Radio, which has a potential audience of more than one billion listeners.

And for the first time, country songs have been recorded in the People's Republic of China. John Beland and Brian Cadd of the Flying Burrito Brothers journeyed to Canton to produce a country album by Zoe, a twenty-year-old Chinese singing star. Songs made famous by Tanya Tucker, Vince Gill, and Reba McEntire were among the tunes recorded behind the Great Wall. How did it go? "They rolled out the red carpet for us, no pun intended," reported Beland. "She [Zoe] sings in three languages, including English, and the album turned out great. It's like contemporary country meets Enya." The country & eastern album on Golden Pony Records will be distributed in China and throughout Southeast Asia.

CMT: Country Music Television's satellite transmitted country-music videos to Latin America and Asia's Pacific Rim while reaching eight million homes through CMT Europe. CMT also launched an advertising blitz in England to increase awareness and viewership among its target audience. The advertising-and-promotion campaign cost a total of $5.1 million.

The growth of country music in Canada sparked a major squabble when the Canadian government removed CMT: Country Music Television from Canada's cable system because of the launching of a new Canadian-owned-and-operated country-music video channel, New Country Network. The battle reached the highest realms of the Canadian and U.S. governments when CMT filed a petition with the U.S. trade representative, seeking punitive action in the matter. The Country Music Association landed in the fray by moving one of its board meetings out of Canada because of CMT's ouster from Canadian cable. The issue was resolved when CMT acquired 20 percent of New

Country Network which, under terms of the agreement, changed its name to CMT-Canada. The twenty-four-hour cable channel reaches more than six million subscribers.

Back home in America, country's TV saturation—by means of CMT, TNN: The Nashville Network, and syndicated and network shows, reached new heights in 1995. *Austin City Limits* began its twentieth season on PBS and continued its tradition of giving country acts a showcase that lasts beyond a song or two. The esteemed show, beamed from Austin, Texas, has helped launch and/or enhance the careers of such artists as Willie Nelson, Jerry Jeff Walker, Michael Martin Murphey, George Strait, Marty Robbins, and George Jones. "The show gives you the ability to do things you could never do on commercial TV," observed Ray Benson, leader of Asleep at the Wheel, who appeared on the first show along with the Texas Playboys. "It allowed us to present ourselves as what we really are because we had thirty full minutes to play our music."

TNN scored high viewer ratings with shows by the Statler Brothers and Marty Stuart and made news with the return of Ralph Emery to host the network's first live daytime talk-and-variety series. The one-hour morning show airs on weekdays from the Opryland Hotel's spectacular Conservatory. The genial host became famous as the overnight deejay on WSM Radio before switching to WSM's TV side and, later, to TNN, where he hosted *Nashville Now* for ten years before Lorianne Crook and Charlie Chase took over.

Crook and Chase, cohorts on the renamed *Music City Tonight*, ended their run in 1995, as conceptual differences between producer Jim Owens and TNN resulted

ON THE RECORD with DOLLY

Obviously, Chet Atkins, Dolly Parton, and Ralph Emery are having no fun at all on one of Ralph Emery's TNN specials.

in the network's shopping for another production company. After spirited competition, dick clark productions—Mr. Clark likes his company low-key and lowercase—was named the new production firm and the search began for the new host or hosts. Crook and Chase meanwhile promised other incarnations for their on-the-air talents.

Country has also permeated network airwaves. Network TV feeds America what it wants, and it wants country TV. Thus networks picked up on the country music boom with CBS's David Letterman, NBC's Jay Leno, and other mega-audience shows scrambling after country acts.

The fast-rising country comedian Jeff Foxworthy, who zoomed to fame with his *You Might Be a Redneck If . . .* album, landed a sitcom on ABC. Foxworthy proved to be one of the most dynamic new talents to break through in

1995, landing four albums on *Billboard*'s pop and country charts. Another favorite of country fans, Marie Osmond, landed an ABC sitcom. Marie's country music heritage includes twenty-one chart singles, four number-one hits, and a CMA Award for her duet with Dan Seals, "Meet Me in Montana."

The annual question from Hank Williams, Jr., "Are you ready for some football?" sets the stage for NFL football for ABC's *Monday Night Football*. The latest football video extravaganza involving Hank was a lavish million-dollar production with a college pom-pom team, five hundred extras, and fireworks. It's a perfect combination of America's favorite pastime and America's favorite music.

Meanwhile, Tribune Entertainment syndicated a series, *The Road*, which combines performances with behind-the-scenes activities and interviews. Among the stars featured were Reba McEntire, John Michael Montgomery, Mary Chapin Carpenter, Travis Tritt, Lari White, and Kathy Mattea.

The Judds provided one of the major media moments of the year with the airing of their miniseries, *Naomi and Wynonna: The Judds*, on NBC. The four-hour show, based on Naomi's hit book *Love Can Build a Bridge*, aired for two hours on Mother's Day, May 14, and concluded on the following night. Naomi practically lived on the set during production in order to ensure, in her words, that the story wouldn't go "Hollyweird." She invited the actresses Viveka David, who played Wynonna, and Kathleen York, who played Naomi, to her Tennessee farm to find out what the Judds are all about. It worked. When a movie executive wanted to change a crucial line in the final scene, not only did

Actresses Kathleen York, who played Naomi, and Viveka David, who starred as Wynonna, effectively capture the magic of the Judds in the NBC miniseries.

Naomi revolt, but so did York. The line stayed in the movie—unchanged.

Another female country-music star—the late and great Dottie West—was portrayed by Michelle Lee in the CBS movie *Big Dreams, Broken Hearts: The Dottie West Story*. The touching story of the Country Sunshine singer, who died in a Nashville car wreck en route to a Grand Ole Opry appearance, included some of her friends cast as themselves. Larry Gatlin (whose career

was launched by West), Chet Atkins, Loretta Lynn, and Dottie's duo partner, Kenny Rogers, all appeared in the movie.

Long-form videos chronicling the lives of the superstars were typified by the ABC Video/Hallway Entertainment tribute tapes capturing performances and personal clips of George Jones, Loretta Lynn, Patsy Cline, Waylon Jennings, and Willie Nelson. The shorter-form videos—those colorful, dramatic ministories that air on CMT, TNN, VH1, and elsewhere—continue to grow in popularity and as a major method for breaking brand-new acts.

On the book beat, the *New York Times* bestseller list, which Ralph Emery and Loretta Lynn scaled in earlier years, welcomed two hot autobiographies—*Reba: My Story* by Reba McEntire and *Dolly: My Life and Other Unfinished Business* by Dolly Parton. Reba's hardcover book, published by Bantam Books, spent fifteen weeks on the *Times* bestseller list and a third printing took it beyond the 600,000 sales mark. *Reba* was released as a paperback in October with an additional update chapter. Dolly's book, published by HarperCollins, spent twelve weeks on the *Times* bestseller list.

Speaking of Reba and Dolly, country culture shock came to Nashville in the form of a new club, Cowboys LaCage. Performing nightly are Reba, Wynonna, the Judds, Lorrie Morgan, Loretta Lynn, Patty Loveless, and Dolly Parton. Well, not *really* Reba and Wy and the others. But it sure does look like them: For the first time in Nashville's history, a female impersonators club centering on country-music stars has opened. Located on Broadway near the Wildhorse Saloon and the Hard Rock Café, Cowboys LaCage attracted large crowds for its premiere season. Some called it controversial; most called it fun, especially when the man who played Reba ripped the wig off the head of the man playing Linda Davis during the McEntire-Davis duet "Does He Love You."

Line dancers at Nashville's already-famous Wildhorse Saloon show their boot-scootin' best moves.

Down the road, the Wildhorse Saloon was *the* place to be in 1995, the Year of the Dance. That's the best way to sum up the explosion of the country-music dance scene. The roaring success of this downtown dance club heralded a national trend of line-dancing clubs, where millions of shuffle-footed fans put their best foot forward. The Official Watermelon Crawl, based on the Tracy Byrd hit, reigned as the favorite line dance. Byrd won two awards for his melonmania at the Country Dance Music Awards, which were held at the Wildhorse Saloon.

The country-music industry became a merchandiser's dream in 1995. The fruits of country-music success brought more money and visibility to such superstars as Alan Jackson, star of a forty-million-dollar performance tour sponsored by Fruit Of The Loom. While many in Jackson's female fan contingent are hoping their lanky hero will model his sponsor's briefest briefs—a la Fruit Of The Loom spokesman-pitcher Jim Palmer—Alan is being secretive about how far he'll go for the campaign, which kicks off in January 1996. A national merchandising-and-promotional program is tied in with Jackson's tour schedule, which begins in New Orleans. The multi-

★ ★

C O U N T R Y , C O U N T R Y ,

Country stars in the movies:
• Randy Travis in *Frank and Jesse*
• Doug Stone in *Gordy*

Country stars on TV:
• Kris Kristofferson plays Abe Lincoln in the Family Channel's movie, *Tad*
• Tom Wopat, former *Dukes of Hazzard* dude, plays Cybill

Shepherd's ex in her CBS sitcom, *Cybill,* and hosts TNN's *Prime Time Country*, which replaced *Music City Tonight*

Country stars turn entrepreneurs:
• George Strait—Pet supplies, including Country Legend shampoo and conditioner and Strait Nutrition Liver Treats for dogs

faceted campaign includes a consumer sweepstakes and national in-store displays.

Need more convincing that country music is big business and big news throughout the world of music? Madonna's publishing company opened a Nashville office in 1995. Victoria Shaw, the vivacious redheaded country singer who created Garth Brooks's number-one hit "The River," is one of the writers.

Welcome to country culture circa 1995.

Although Alan Jackson looks great in his Fruit Of The Loom sweat-shirt touting the company that sponsored his forty-million-dollar tour, his female fans were hoping he might model the company's briefs.

★ ★

E V E R Y W H E R E !

- Tanya Tucker—Salsa that's feisty as Tanya herself
- Reba McEntire—The Reba Visa card
- Reba McEntire, Vince Gill, & other stars—Country Star Restaurant chain, known for their chile, burgers, and ribs
- Marty Stuart & Garth Brooks—Music City stores, which sell T-shirts and other memorabilia

- Alabama—Grocery products, named after the group, such as jambalaya and chicken & dumplings
- Kenny Rogers—*Showboat Branson Belle*, a 270-foot paddle wheeler that carries passengers seeking meals and music on Table Rock Lake in Branson, Missouri

F A N

F A I R

*Tim McGraw reaches out
and touches some of his fans—a
frequent occurrence during
Fan Fair's close encounters
of the best kind.*

'95

THE FAIREST OF THEM ALL

Take 24,000 country-music fans from 28 countries, add 183 superstar-filled exhibition booths, blend in hot performances by 86 acts, stir for 6 days at 97 degrees, and you've got 1995's International Country Music Fan Fair. It's the recipe for a country-music lover's version of heaven on earth. Perhaps remembering that fan is short for fanatic, these talent-seeking tourists spent more than $9 million, snapped more than 70,000 photos, and ate 13,000 pounds of barbecue prepared by the Odessa, Texas, Chuck Wagon Gang.

Held at the Tennessee State Fairgrounds in Nashville, the twenty-fourth annual Fan Fair was once again a sold-out, stellar, star-studded songfest and lovefest. Sponsored by the Grand Ole Opry and the Country Music Association, Fan Fair draws not only the fans but an international press corps numbering in the hundreds, which chronicles this unique annual bonding session between country stars and those die-hard fans who make them, and keep them, stars.

The historic onstage reunion of Tammy Wynette and George Jones provided one of the magical moments of Fan Fair '95.

This year Tim McGraw kicked it all off with a red-hot performance at the Curb Records Show, and those hilarious would-be cowboys, Riders in the Sky, closed down the proceedings five days later. In between was a live, nonstop, boot-stompin', star-studded country jukebox. The record-label–sponsored performances took place on twin main stages in front of the Nashville Speedway grandstand. While an act performed on one stage, the next artist and band set up on the adjoining stage to allow nonstop musical action.

The MCA/Decca Records Show on Tuesday evening provided the top trio of Fan Fair—George, Tammy, and Wy. Although a typical summer thunderstorm rumbled through, the fans stayed. When George Jones and Tammy Wynette—former singing partners, former husband and wife, former combatants during and after their marital breakup—walked onstage together, the fans rose as one to give them a standing ovation, cheering the memories, the music, the thought that reconciliation is possible both onstage and off. Their four-song set didn't disappoint, especially with the reprise of their 1976 number-one hit, "Golden Ring." Another standing ovation accompanied the departure of country's all-time coolest couple from the stage.

Wynonna, performing for the first time since having a baby in 1994, also electrified the audience—and got a thrill herself. "I've been sitting at home, and it's good to be singing again," Wy told the crowd. "Music can be the true healer." Mix the reunion of George and

Neal McCoy takes his performance to new heights by climbing the scaffolding during his rousing Fan Fair appearance.

Tammy, and the comeback of Wynonna, and add the debuts of brilliant new singers assaulting the charts for the first time, and you've got a Fan Fair that will go down with the best of them.

Neal McCoy took his singing to new heights at the Atlantic Records Show when he climbed the scaffolding during one of the wildest performances of Fan Fair, and Giant's Doug Supernaw thrilled his fans by wandering among them while singing a song made popular by David Allan Coe, "You Never Even Called Me by My Name," and letting some of the audience members sing the chorus. Attempt to sing the chorus might be a better description.

David Lee Murphy, during his Fan Fair debut at MCA's show, made a telling comment to the audience: "Even though this is my first performance here, I'm no stranger to Fan Fair. Last year I was standing right out there with you." That's how fast country music is moving nowadays.

Another highlight was John Berry, one year removed from his return to the stage after brain surgery. He thrilled the crowd with an energetic set that had his

Celebrating the anniversary of his return to the stage after brain surgery, a healthier and happier John Berry marks the moment with his soulful music.

booming voice bouncing off the rafters. Executives from Capitol Records/Nashville surprised him with a platinum album, signifying sales of one million for his debut album. And to think, just a year earlier, the singer was worried about whether he would ever see 1995.

Billy Ray Cyrus was back, again igniting the fans, and Shania Twain, the fastest-rising country star since Billy Ray, put on a performance as dazzling as her beauty. If the remote control had been on mute, fans would have thought they were watching a beauty contest, with such heartthrobs as Shania, Ronna Reeves, Holly Dunn, Patty Loveless, Faith Hill, Chely Wright, Amie Comeaux, Bobbie Cryner, and Kathy Mattea performing.

Female fans weren't left without their hunkabilly delights. Cyrus, Jackson, McGraw, McCoy, and Murphy were joined by such handsome talents as George Ducas, Tracy Byrd, Mark Chesnutt, David Ball, Tracy Lawrence, Steve Wariner, James House, Ken Mellons, Collin Raye, Woody Lee, Mark Collie, Rick Trevino, and crowd favorites Kix Brooks and Ronnie Dunn.

Fan Fair is much more than stage performances: it's the one-on-one encounters between fan and star. And where those happen is the nirvana of the exhibition halls— several one-story buildings on the fairground where fans meet, greet, and hug their favorite country stars, get their autographs, and take advantage of the photo opportunities. The stars' fan clubs put in the hard work of conceptualizing and constructing the exhibition and manning many of the colorful booths. Other booths are sponsored by record companies, TNN, CMT, the Grand Ole Opry, country music magazines, and other country-oriented enterprises.

Wandering down these packed corridors is an exercise in what country music is all about. It's a face-to-face, one-on-one, star-meets-fan, fan-meets-star paradise. Fan Fair–goers tote cameras for the photos, pens for the autographs, and sacks for the merchandise, the autographed mementos, and the record albums, which they purchase at the on-site record store, where the top three sellers of 1995 were Wade Hayes, Shania Twain, and Alan Jackson.

The fans themselves are as colorful as Porter Wagoner's jackets. They wear T-shirts, buttons, and pins hawking their favorite acts. They buy Fan Fair caps. Some sport tattoos depicting their favorite artist. They range from babies to grandparents; one of the latter—an eighty-something fellow—wore a T-shirt proclaiming ROWDY BUNCH. Some are college kids, some are dropouts. They're polite and persistent, diverse in dress and dialect. And they

Vince Gill proves just how close fans can get to their superstar favorites during Fan Fair's booth action.

"It's feisty!" proclaim the salsa signs at Tanya Tucker's booth. Does that apply to the salsa, Tanya, or both?

all have one thing in common: they love their country music and the writers and singers who have made it a vital part of their lives.

From preteens to grandmothers, the fans flock through the corridors, seeking—and in most cases finding—that heavenly moment with their favorite artist. It's a chance to get Alan Jackson's autograph and cuddle up for a photo with Vince Gill. Or pose with Tanya Tucker as she hawks her Tanya Tucker salsa in a building where the air conditioning has temporarily gone out, yet nobody cares because it's packed with a galaxy of stars. Anyone who wants to know what Janie Fricke is up to nowadays can just ask her. She's signing autographs at booth 163.

Screams of joy and mini-stampedes are commonplace as fans greet the stars arriving for their booth appearances. Some fans wait in line for four or five hours to meet their favorites. And some performers spend hours greeting and signing and posing. Lesser-known acts draw shorter lines, but they still draw attention—after all, they could be the Garths or the Rebas of the future.

Predictably, this year's lines at Vince Gill's booth became long when the public-address system announced he was there and signing. Vince Gill had a small and understated booth—to match his ego and his persona. Billy Dean was swamped by admirers when he appeared, and extra-long lines queued up for Marty Stuart and Little Texas. Tanya Tucker was as hot as her salsa in her booth, which bore the legend for both her product and herself: IT'S FEISTY!

A rocking chair added reality to Ty Herndon's re-creation of a front porch. Showing a sense of humor, the Bellamy Brothers drew attention to their single "Big Hair" with a hair-salon-theme booth displaying Polaroid photos of big-haired fans who allowed the Bellamys to judge their hairdos on "hair height, width, and overall obnoxiousness."

Sammy Kershaw took advantage of the fun atmosphere to announce to his fans—especially the ones from his home state—"I'm going to run for gover-nor of Louisiana someday, and I'm going to win!" Doug Supernaw gave his fans butt patches and was more than happy to help pat them on. Doug Stone gave emphasis to his last name by utilizing an early Flintstones decor.

One of the biggest draws—especially when the star was there—was the Billy Ray Cyrus "BRC Spirit" exhibit. Beneath a REDNECK HEAVEN TOUR sign, a paint-ing showed such long-gone and lamented singers as Patsy Cline, Conway Twitty, Keith Whitley, and Elvis Presley in a heaven-sent honky-tonk. The only rules posted were: NO CUSSING, FUSSING, FIGHTING—JUST SINGING.

Known for his elaborate sets, Alan Jackson maintained his reputation with the Jackson Junction Café, a fifties-era soda

Lee Roy Parnell plays a winning hand with his number-one booth that plugs his new album.

shop with a painting depicting happy diners and classic smiling waitresses. Pam Tillis had fun with two definitions of fan in her Pam Tillis Fan Shoppe. There for all the fans to see was an exhibit of fans—the cooling kind—from antique feather fans to electric ones.

Reba McEntire recalled with a laugh her first Fan Fair appearance, in 1976. Her first Mercury Records release had spent only five weeks on the Billboard Hot Country Singles chart, reaching only eighty-eight on the top one hundred. "My mother was standing behind me in the booth, and we saw all these long lines for other singers, but nobody was coming up for my autograph. I wanted her to be proud of me, but both of us were about to cry because no fan even approached me. Finally this middle-aged couple came up to me, and did I get excited! I took my Sharpie pen out and was ready to autograph a picture when the man asked me, 'Ma'am, could you tell me how to get to the rest room?' That was a dark moment in my career." Reba doesn't have that problem anymore, but she'll never forget her first Fan Fair.

There was friendly competition for the best booth title. The 1995 winner was Lee Roy Parnell, whose booth boosted his new album, *We All Get Lucky Sometimes*. It featured such gambling paraphernalia as huge dice, dominoes, and a full-house deck of cards. Faith Hill came up with the idea of constructing a replica of her barn, complete with saddles, a wagon wheel, and plenty of hay—in bales and scattered on the floor. It was good enough for second place. The third-place ribbon went to Clay Walker's booth, which was designed like the front of a movie theater, the Melrose Cinema, with the marquee advertising NOW PLAYING . . . CLAY WALKER.

"I've got it!" yells Doug Supernaw, who also hammered a home run during the City of Hope benefit softball game, a highlight of Fan Fair Week.

Scores of peripheral activities surround Fan Fair Week. This year, ending the day before Fan Fair started, Nashville's annual Summer Lights Festival was held. It drew more than 124,000 music devotees—fans of all types of music—including many who would attend Fan Fair. Among the country acts that played the block-party fest in downtown Nashville were Chet Atkins, Suzy Bogguss, Ronnie Milsap, Clay Walker, Lee Greenwood, Billy Dean, Little Texas, Shelby Lynne, Kim Carnes, Steve Kolander, Toby Keith, and John Michael Montgomery.

Another pre–Fan Fair event was the annual City of Hope Celebrity Softball Game at Greer Stadium, home of the Nashville Sounds, the triple-A team of the Chicago White Sox. Benefiting the City of Hope National Medical Center and Beckman Research

Institute, the game saw two country-music all-star teams battle each other for bragging rights. After Martina McBride sang the national anthem, it was play ball for such superstars as Tanya Tucker, Vince Gill, Billy Ray Cyrus, Clint Black, Michelle Wright, Joe Diffie, Doug Supernaw, Kathy Mattea, and Daron Norwood.

Another Fan Fair Week charity event, Ride for Life, benefited the Muscular Dystrophy Association. Country music's biking brethren—ranging from George Jones to Lee Roy Parnell—rode out to Percy Priest Lake, where they performed for seven thousand fans. It was Harley heaven for such cycle enthusiasts as Steve Earle, Brooks & Dunn, and Larry Stewart.

The June 5 TNN/Music City News Awards were also held during Fan Fair, with Alan Jackson carting off the largest number of trophies. He took home a total of five awards—Album of the Year, Song of the Year, Vocal Collaboration (with George Jones), Male Artist, and Entertainer of the Year.

As is the case at every Fan Fair, fan-club parties abounded all week long. Doug Supernaw took his fans to Tex's Western Bar-B-Q for a Texas-style beef-brisket feast. Alan Jackson performed for twenty-five hundred of his fans at the Tennessee Performing Arts Center. And at their party, Tracy Byrd and Toby Keith played a game of softball before performing for the crowd. Reba McEntire once again spent hours greeting her fans and signing autographs at the Municipal Auditorium. She's been known to work through the night, until the last auto-graph has been signed.

A highlight of Joe Diffie's party at 328 Performance Hall was the wedding of Scott Beebe and Jonni Behm of Westfield, Pennsylvania, who got married onstage. And then they danced to Joe's performance of "So Help Me Girl."

All week thousands of journalists who had traveled across the globe recorded the best of this fest for those who hadn't been able to get to Fan Fair themselves. One building—accessible by pass only—was used for this international press contingent. Private booths were set aside for interviews of the stars by radio, TV, and print reporters. Fans gathered outside the building as stars arrived in their limos and cars and darted inside for their interviews.

Fans, artists, record producers, journalists—a lot of people attend Fan Fair each year. Just how do Fan Fair coordinators prepare food for so many hungry people? Texas style! At a giant outdoor, roofed pavilion, thousands of the fans chowed down on Texas barbecue, cole slaw, beans, pickles, and iced tea, served by the Odessa, Texas, Chuck Wagon Gang.

After the week's blur of activities and performances, worn out but won over fans headed back home. Back to California, New York, Maine, Oregon, and Florida, back to England, Japan, Germany, Canada, and twenty-three other countries. They carried with them priceless photographs and autographs that they will cherish forever, memories of meeting their favorite star face-to-face and watching a week's worth of the finest country talent money can buy. And many of those fans, planning another pilgrimage to the capital of country music, circled the dates of Fan Fair 1996: June 10 to 16, 1996— International Country Music Fan Fair's twenty-fifth anniversary celebration.

FAN FAIR 1995

★ **JUNE 5**
The Bluegrass Show
featuring Bill Monroe

★ **JUNE 6**
Morning: Curb Show,
featuring Junior Brown,
Hank Williams, Jr.,
and Tim McGraw
Afternoon: Mercury
Show, featuring Billy Ray
Cyrus, Shania Twain, and
Sammy Kershaw
Evening: MCA and
Decca Show, featuring
Mark Chesnutt, Tracy
Byrd, Wynonna, and
George Jones and Tammy
Wynette

★ **JUNE 7**
Morning: Liberty and
Patriot Show, featuring
John Berry, Chris LeDoux,
and George Ducas
Afternoon:
Warner/Reprise and
Asylum Show, featuring
Faith Hill, David Ball, and
Bryan White
Evening: RCA and BNA
Show, featuring Lari
White, Kenny Chesney,
and Alabama

★ **JUNE 8**
Morning: Atlantic and
Giant Show, featuring
Tracy Lawrence, Clay
Walker, and Neal McCoy
Afternoon: Arista and
Career Show, featuring
Alan Jackson, Lee Roy
Parnell, and the Tractors
Evening: Columbia and
Epic Show, featuring Joe
Diffie, Patty Loveless, and
Collin Raye

★ **JUNE 9**
Polydor/Nashville Show,
featuring Toby Keith,
Chely Wright, and
Davis Daniel

Multi-Label Show,
featuring Holly Dunn
(River North), Western
Flyer (Step One),
Sweethearts of the Rodeo
(Sugar Hill), and Alison
Krauss (Rounder Records)

★ **JUNE 10**
Grand Masters Fiddling
Championship at
Opryland USA

2 0 0 1

A SONG

Shania Twain:
down-home diva.

ODYSSEY

4

SEVEN WHO'LL MAKE IT

Like life itself, country music is cyclical. A year or two may slide by without the thrill of discovering a new voice, a new personality, a vibrant new addition to the fertile landscape that nurtures lasting careers in the whirl of country music. During the urban-cowboy craze in the early eighties, the industry bowed down to the false gods of pop music. Plasticized, overproduced, over-thought, pretentious music fooled the masses for a few years. Then Wall Street bankers and Brooklyn lawyers discovered that their newly purchased cowboy boots hurt like hell until they were broken in. Meanwhile, as millions of country-music fans discovered that country Muzak drains the heart, soul, and power from their beloved art form, country took a justifiable dive.

Thankfully, the urban-cowboy phase died as quickly as it was born, but in the meantime many fresh, new acts were lost in the saccharine-laced gold rush. Then George Strait came along and provided a handsome new face and dynamite new traditional country voice to lead the way and bridge the gap until a new breed of country performers arrived on the scene. As the Wall Street and Brooklyn cowboys were dispatching those painful boots to the nearest Salvation Army store, Strait scored his first number-one hit, "Fool Hearted Memory," in 1982. On the female side, Reba McEntire, a country-to-the-core singer who had been plugging away with records since 1976, enjoyed her first number one in the same year. Ironically, in 1985, Randy Travis released "1982," a song that took him to the top ten. The next year "On the Other Hand" delivered him the number-one spot and further ignited the return to country's traditional roots that continues to this day.

The last few years have seen country's up cycle in overdrive. Alan Jackson, Garth Brooks, and Clint Black were unknown a decade ago but are now considered established superstars. On their heels came a new generation of multimillion-sellers, like Tracy Byrd, John Michael Montgomery, and Brooks & Dunn. Then there are the newest performers making their first big splash on the country—and sometimes pop—charts.

The rich mother lode of country-music talent has provided many candidates for an extended career in this highly competitive field. Their backgrounds, philosophies, and voices differ. But they're linked by a common thread of endless talent and boundless determination to make it to the top and stay there. The seven profiled below should be enjoying success on the airwaves and music charts five years from now, when country music enters the magical year of 2001.

JOHN BERRY. John has lived the lyrics of a country-music-from-tragedy-to-the-top ballad. Try this. After years of playing clubs in his home region of Athens, Georgia, John won over the jaded broadcasters at the 1994 Country Radio Seminar with his solo version of "Your Love Amazes Me." He barely remembers performing, but he does remember the blinding headaches, exhaustion, and weight loss he was experiencing.

John Berry, recovered from life-threatening brain surgery, gratefully serenades his son Sean Thomas on the porch of his farmhouse near Athens, Georgia.

At about the same time, Berry's wife and backup singer, Robin, entered the hospital for the birth of their second child. Sean Thomas was born in perfect health, but Sean Thomas's father couldn't even work up enthusiasm for his first-born son. He nearly collapsed in a hospital hallway and called for a doctor.

An examination revealed bad news: a growth on John's brain. Berry underwent five hours of painfully delicate and dangerous surgery to remove the tumor, which, mercifully, turned out to be benign. As his single hit number one, the focus was on remaining alive. His life was in the balance, but the operation was a success.

A few months later he made his return to the stage at Fan Fair, getting a hug from emcee Charlie Daniels and performing an acoustic version of "Your Love Amazes Me" to a standing ovation. John Berry's recovery amazed everyone.

His first album went gold, his second album started climbing the charts, and a second son, Caelan James, was born, joining brother Sean Thomas and sister TaylorMarie in a family that has much to be thankful for.

MARTINA McBRIDE. What a year for the woman from the Land of Oz! The native of Sharon, Kansas, winner of Country Music Association's Video of the Year honor in 1994, continued her climb toward the upper reaches of country-music stardom in 1995. Her second album on RCA Records, *The Way That I Am*, soared to platinum status, bursting new barriers for the beautiful thrush, whose "Independence Day" will go down as an anthem for the victims of abusive relationships.

Martina started her show-business career as a T-shirt salesperson for Garth Brooks, the superstar who also

Martina McBride, the beautiful woman from the Land of Oz, is paving her own gold and platinum brick road to the land where everything is colorful and country.

employed Martina's husband and sound engineer, John McBride, as his production manager. Now Martina is not letting motherhood slow down her skyrocketing career. Delaney Katharine, born over the 1994 Christmas holidays, is going along on her mother's ride to fame. Their roomy Baby Bus accommodates Martina, John, and Delaney, whose traveling digs include a crib, rocker, and playpen. All three—mother, father, and daughter—confront the rigorous road schedule. Like the yellow brick road to Oz, Martina's highway is paved with gold.

LEE ROY PARNELL. "This is the guy I really want to break," said Tim DuBois, chief of Arista Records/Nashville. The man who has given country music such great acts as Restless Heart, Alan Jackson, and the

Lee Roy Parnell, one of the most respected new singer-instrumentalists in Nashville, enjoys swapping licks with his idol, Merle Haggard.

Tractors stubbornly hung in with Lee Roy through some unimpressive chart years. His perseverance paid off as Lee Roy's album *We All Get Lucky Sometimes* dramatically hit the charts and yielded his first number-one hit, "A Little Bit of You," making 1995 a landmark year for the country singer from Abilene, Texas.

Lee Roy is another of those "overnight successes" who spend a decade or two honing their craft in smoky clubs and boisterous honky-tonks before reaching the top. He moved to Nashville in 1987, gained his first chart record three years later, and reached the pinnacle of country-music success five years after that.

A disciple of Texas swing king Bob Wills, Lee Roy used the fiddle of the late Country Music Hall of Fame great when recording "A Little Bit of You." A Wills family member gave Lee Roy the fiddle as a gift, and Parnell treats it like the Holy Grail. He even built a shrine to it in the recording studio.

Lee Roy's hearty blend of country, rock, blues, and western swing derives from such influences as Merle Haggard, Muddy Waters, and the Allman Brothers. Besides his skills as a singer, Lee Roy is one of the best slide-guitar players in the business.

THE MAVERICKS. Many blue highways and interstates lead to Nashville and music-business victory, but one of the strangest of these, and one of the longest, was traveled by the Mavericks.

The Mavericks created a buzz in the early nineties while playing in country-music clubs in the Miami area. Several record companies sent representatives to check out the hot new band with a Cuban connection (thanks to lead singer Raul Malo), but decided not to sign the four-man group because they couldn't find a chart niche for it.

MCA Records finally took a chance, signed the Florida foursome, and released the album *From Hell to Paradise* in 1992. The album's scattered style confused radio programmers, who focused on the "countriest" of the songs, the Hank Williams evergreen "Hey, Good Lookin'." The single spent a grand total of one week on the charts.

Record-company executives and the group members themselves fine-tuned their efforts, knowing the second album would be their last unless airplay and sales improved. It took longer than usual, but *What a Crying Shame* became the Mavericks' breakthrough album, spawning such hit singles as "O What a Thrill," "I Should Have Been True," and the title track.

From the road less traveled to the road to the platinum plateau, the Mavericks—Raul Malo, guitarist Nick Kane, bassist Robert Reynolds, and drummer Paul Deakin—won their first top honors in 1995 when the Academy of Country Music named them Top New Vocal Group and Top Vocal Group.

SHANIA TWAIN. No newcomer jumped to the top of the charts in 1995 with more speed and more spectacle than the gorgeous Shania Twain. No one journeyed farther to make a video than Shania, who traveled to the pyramids and other ancient monuments of Egypt for a stunning backdrop. And no one in Nashville believes anything can stop the Canadian beauty from becoming one of the new superstars of country music.

Her album on Mercury/Nashville Records, *The Woman in Me*, leaped to number one on *Billboard*'s Top Country Albums chart and placed in the top ten on the magazine's Pop Album chart. Shania's first single, the saucy "Whose Bed Have Your Boots Been Under," also made her queen of the charts. She touched all the number-one bases when her video for "Any Man of Mine" reached the top of CMT's ranking.

Twain, from Windsor, Ontario, started singing professionally at the age of eight and grew as an entertainer while performing as a roadhouse singer. Her job at the

Deerhurst Resort in northern Ontario helped her and her siblings survive the tragic aftermath of their parents' death in a car accident when Shania was twenty-one. Deerhurst was also where Shania auditioned for her record contract and where she married John "Mutt" Lange, who produces her records (and has produced such pop acts as Bryan Adams and Michael Bolton).

Twain composes alone and in collaboration with her husband. The talented, beautiful, and driven singer-songwriter has promoted her work in the United States and overseas, thus ensuring that her career will thrive for years to come.

WADE HAYES. "Old enough to know better, still too young to care" are lyrics that helped take young Wade Hayes to the top of the country charts. The song—written by Wade and veteran cleffer Chick Rains—climbed

Wade Hayes follows the powerful Oklahoma pathways to stardom blazed by Reba McEntire, Garth Brooks, and Vince Gill.

to number one and fulfilled the dreams of Wade's father, who once tried to snag the golden ring on the country merry-go-round.

Growing up in a musical household in Bethel Acres, Oklahoma, Wade followed the footsteps of his father, who was a regional singing favorite. He learned the joys of entertaining an audience. When the family moved to Nashville after his father signed an independent record deal, Wade learned the sometimes cruel realities of show-business life. The deal fell through, and the hardships that resulted after the family moved back to Oklahoma made Wade wary of the dark side of the business.

"My family taught me to always work hard," commented Wade, who continued to pursue the muse of music after his return to the Sooner State. He dropped out of college to chase his own musical dreams and, despite his misgivings about his father's misfortunes in Nashville, decided to give it a try.

Wade met the producer Don Cook while sitting in as a guitarist at a showcase, and he soon began writing with Chick Rains, a Cook associate. Their song "I'm Still Dancin' with You" won Wade a publishing deal and a recording contract—all within a three-day period. As his career blossomed, Wade began living his father's dreams.

DAVID BALL. It's the song that other country stars love to sing. Many of them—including Faith Hill, John Michael Montgomery, Alan Jackson, and Neal McCoy have sung it at their concerts, though perhaps only singing the memorable in-your-face first line, "Yes, I admit, I've got a thinkin' problem."

Like some of country's biggest songs, "Thinkin' Problem" wasn't an instant hit. "I always thought it

David Ball suffered a "Thinkin' Problem" when he auditioned for a record label executive at a Nashville honky-tonk.

would be a big hit," David revealed, "but it kind of sat around and didn't do anything for a couple years. When I had a chance to make a record, I went back and got it because that's the one I had always wanted to record."

Born in Rock Hill, South Carolina, David learned to play guitar when he was only seven years old. He wrote songs in grade school and during his high school years played with musicians in the Spartanburg area. In the mid-seventies, he moved to the creative hot spot of Austin, Texas, with Uncle Walt's Band, a trio. David assimilated the rich Texas aura of Bob Wills and

Names to watch for ... and their hits ...

★ Rhett Akins   "That Ain't My Truck"
★ Jeff Carson   "Not on Your Love"
★ Kenny Chesney   "All I Need to Know"
★ Terri Clark   "Better Things to Do"
★ Mark Collie   "Even the Man in the Moon Is Crying"
★ Wesley Dennis   "Who's Counting"
★ Diamond Rio   "Meet in the Middle"
★ George Ducas   "Lipstick Promises"
★ Emilio   "It's Not the End of the World"
★ Ty England   "Should've Asked Her Faster"
★ Radney Foster   "Nobody Wins"
★ Ty Herndon   "What Mattered Most"
★ Little Texas   "Some Guys Have All the Love"
★ Lonestar   "Tequila Talkin' "
★ Shelby Lynn   "I'm Not the One"
★ Ken Mellons   "Jukebox Junkie"
★ Billy Montana   "Didn't Have You"
★ David Lee Murphy   "Dust on the Bottle"
★ Daron Norwood   "Bad Dog, No Biscuit"
★ Daryle Singletary   "I Let Her Lie"
★ Doug Stone   "I'd Be Better Off in a Pine Box"
★ Doug Supernaw   "I Don't Call Him Daddy"
★ Rick Trevino   "Bobbie Ann Mason"
★ Ron Wallace   "I'm Listening Now"
★ Bryan White   "Someone Else's Star"
★ Lari White   "What a Woman Wants"
★ Michelle Wright   "Take It Like a Man"

... and their hit albums

★ BlackHawk   *Strong Enough*
★ Junior Brown   *Junior High*
★ Jeff Foxworthy   *You Might Be a Redneck If . . .*
★ James House   *Days Gone By*
★ Toby Keith   *Boomtown*
★ Alison Krauss   *Now That I've Found You: A Collection*
★ Neal McCoy   *You Gotta Love That*
★ Perfect Stranger   *You Have the Right to Remain Silent*
★ Chely Wright   *Woman in the Moon*

George Jones before moving to Nashville in the late eighties.

The producer Blake Chancey discovered David when the singer was performing in a tiny Music Row honky-tonk, the Idle Hour Tavern, in the past a favorite haunt of Roger Miller, Willie Nelson, and Kris Kristofferson. Chancey came back with an executive from Warner Bros. Records for a show David will never forget: "They came in and I just sat and sang while a cab driver was in there trying to sell everyone tennis shoes he looted from a tractor-trailer wreck on the interstate."

Not only did Chancey and the Warner Bros. executive get some nice tennis shoes, but they also got a damned fine singer, who gave them one of the most memorable country songs in history and followed "Thinkin' Problem" with more hits in 1995.

Mark down these seven as sure superstars of the future. That's not ruling out major success from other bright new talents who also might gain superstar status. Names like Toby Keith, Kenny Chesney, and others are all likely candidates for country-music superstardom.

There's a lot of competition, and there's more talent than has ever crashed the country charts at one time. Many of these musicians are now joining that exclusive country club of multimillion-sellers.

"Hello, Tracy Byrd. Hello, Mark Chesnutt. Hello, Tim McGraw. My name is Shania Twain. Do y'all have room in there for me? I'm coming in."

MILLION-
SELLERS

5

TAKING IT TO THE TOP

The throng of impressive new talent has vaulted to a new plateau of gold and platinum success within the last year or two. Although some will drop out, some will persevere and conquer the highly competitive world of country-music stardom. Some of these acts might be trivia questions in the year of 2000. Others will be at the top of the heap.

Let's look at some of those who populate this region and should move to higher realms—the new generation of multimillion-sellers. These acts have moved a step beyond the newcomers and a step closer to superstardom on that long, challenging stairway to the top echelon of country-music performers.

MARK CHESNUTT. If Mark could survive "that night" at a Texas honky-tonk, he can survive any career challenge that lies ahead. "That night" took place when Mark was a teenager playing one of those rowdy, smoky music saloons. As waiters hustled greasy food and potent drinks to the tables, Mark tried to outsing the noise of the crowd and gain at least a little attention and, God knows, just a little bit of applause. Usually, applause never came as Mark poured his heart and soul into his music. But this night, as he finished a song he heard someone clapping. Stunned, he gazed through the haze into the darkened room, trying to find the source of the sound.

"Thank you very much," he said into the darkness. But when his eyes finally focused on the clapping man, his heart dipped as he saw what was happening. The man was slapping the bottom of his ketchup bottle, garnishing his cheeseburger.

That incident would have ended the career of many a lesser soul, but Chesnutt kept on, honing his craft and hoping for better times to come. And they came. They saw. He conquered.

Mark had recorded two songs for a small record company with little success, but he eventually gained the attention of MCA Records executive Tony Brown with a tape of "Too Cold at Home." Brown and other MCA officials journeyed to Beaumont, Texas, to catch Mark in action. They came away impressed—and with a brand-new artist. "Too Cold at Home" became his first single and zoomed to number three, and his second, "Brother Jukebox," went to number one. Mark's first three MCA albums have gone platinum and his fourth album, *Wings*, has climbed into the golden territory.

Like Tracy Byrd and Clay Walker, Mark is one of those tremendous Texas talents hailing from Beaumont. His idols include Merle Haggard, George Jones, and Elvis Presley. Like any Elvis fan, Mark collects anything associated with the idol: records, tapes, photos, books, and other souvenirs. The Decca Records artist even makes periodic pilgrimages to Graceland in Memphis.

Two highlights of this memorable year for Mark: During a Memphis trip, he met the legendary Sun Records producer Sam Phillips, who discovered such great talents as Elvis, Johnny Cash, Jerry Lee Lewis, and Carl Perkins. And at Nashville's Ryman Auditorium, he was honored with a This Is Your Life tribute. Family, friends, and music-business leaders paid homage to the shy, fast-rising star.

TRACY BYRD. Tracy Byrd celebrated the platinum success of his MCA Records album *No Ordinary Man* by treating his entire band and road crew to a fun-filled fishing excursion aboard the eighty-five-foot "house barge" the *Chandeleur Discovery*. Byrd and crew ventured out from the Cypress Cove Marina in Venice, Louisiana, heading toward the Chandeleurs, a chain of islands in the Gulf of Mexico. Three days later they returned with hundreds of fish, some sunburns, and many stories.

Born in Vidor, Texas, Tracy was weaned on the music of Bob Wills, Merle Haggard, and Ray Price. He played the dance clubs and honky-tonks, including a stint with the house band led by Mark Chesnutt at the late and great Beaumont club Cutter's. When Chesnutt headed for Nashville, Byrd took over his Cutter's chores. Following a Nashville showcase and a nerve-shattering private solo performance for MCA Records chiefs Bruce Hinton and Tony Brown, Tracy was signed to MCA.

In 1995, "Keeper of the Stars" earned the tall Texan a Country Music Association nomination for Single of the Year. He won new fans while appearing on the hot Reba McEntire tour and watched his newest album jump to number six on *Billboard*'s Top Country Albums chart.

Though Tracy's hectic schedule keeps him on the road most of the year, he did manage to squeeze in some favorite sporting activities, and even sponsored his own fishing tournament near Beaumont that benefitted the March of Dimes.

Tracy Byrd's biggest catch of his Chandeleur Islands fishing trip—a 169-pound steel guitarist, Marc Matoska.

Tracy also went hunting and fishing in Alaska after playing a concert there and took a Caribbean cruise with his wife, Michelle.

A splendid mix of song and sports success made 1995 the best year of Tracy's career and life so far. And his latest album, *Love Lessons*, should propel his fame and fortune even higher in 1996.

FAITH HILL. This was a year to remember for one of the most beautiful women to appear on country music's landscape. The year began with the frightening realization that she needed throat surgery to seal a dilated blood vessel. The trauma of undergoing that surgery was followed by seventy-five days of silence, but ended with the joy in learning that the career-threatening problem had been successfully treated. Add to that her first platinum album, *Take Me As I Am*. And, for the pièce de résistance, she broke her postsurgery silence to say yes to a marriage proposal from her record producer, Scott Hendricks, currently the chief of Capitol Records/Nashville.

The Warner Bros. Records artist, born Audrey Faith Perry in Star, Mississippi, flashes radiant beauty and a dramatic depth of talent. She grew up idolizing Tammy Wynette, Loretta Lynn, Patsy Cline, and Elvis Presley—three country greats and one rock icon who have greatly influenced the new generation of country artists.

The year of ups and downs ended on a positive note with Faith's return to the concert stage and recording studio. She released her second album, *It Matters to Me*, and it started that upward chart climb, promising more gold and platinum awards ahead.

The lovely lady, who's keeping the faith, revealed how she received her name: "I was adopted and my parents

had believed they would eventually find a little girl. They felt with the faith they had that their dreams would come true."

Her parents' dreams did come true. And now the dreams of Faith Hill are also coming true . . . on record and in romance.

BROOKS & DUNN. Kix Brooks and Ronnie Dunn, the hottest duo in country music, are just one notch away from being in the highest rank of country-music superstars. Take this for starters: three platinum albums; vocal-duo awards from the Country Music Association, TNN/Music City News, and the Academy of Country Music (which also presented them with single and album honors); and a Grammy Award for Best Country Vocal Performance.

But Kix Brooks, a native of Shreveport, Louisiana, and Ronnie Dunn, who was born in Coleman, Texas, and later moved to Tulsa, Oklahoma, are not content with the status quo. "We want our level of entertainment and our show to be in the same ballpark with Garth, Alan, Vince, and Reba," explained Kix. Added his singing partner, "It's evolved to where we don't even look at the duo category anymore." That can be translated as "One day we want to win Entertainer of the Year."

That day may be coming soon; Brooks & Dunn have worked hard for it, playing the tiny clubs and honky-tonks in their home states. They began writing together after brief flings as solo artists brought them both to Nashville. Signed to Arista Records, Brooks & Dunn came out of the box in 1991 with a number-one hit, "Brand New Man." The next year "Boot Scootin' Boogie" helped launch the popularity of the line-dancing craze and became the duo's fourth consecutive number-one record.

Dust off that Entertainer of the Year Award. Engrave the names. It'll soon belong to Brooks & Dunn.

TIM McGRAW. Nobody has to tell Tim McGraw to get a life. He has one. A very interesting one. How about growing up idolizing a major-league baseball star and eventually discovering that he is your father? That happened when Tim learned that Tug McGraw, the famed New York Mets pitcher, is his father. Tim was the product of a summer romance between his mother, who had just graduated from high school, and Tug, who was then a minor-league ballplayer. When Tim's mother later married, the youngster grew up thinking his step-dad was his real father. When they divorced, Tim was told the truth, and, at age eleven, met his real father for the first time. Through the years they finally bonded as father and son and enjoy spending time together.

McGraw inherited his father's athletic skills and thirst for competition, only in a different field of dreams. The Curb Records artist was born and raised in Start, Louisiana. He attended Northeast Louisiana University on sports scholarships, but music became his first love and, eventually, his path to stardom.

Signed to Curb in 1992, Tim released three singles from his first album that achieved little acclaim or chart action through 1993. Unlike his pitcher-father, he didn't want a no-hit career. Come 1994, his show-business career took off like a home-run ball hit out of the park. From a baseball diamond to a platinum album, Tim's remarkable rise to country-music stardom began with his album *Not a Moment Too Soon*. Five million copies later, Tim is atop the whirl of country music.

Just like a finely tuned athlete, McGraw keeps looking ahead. His goal for 1996: "Keep improving. I have to pay close attention to my career and make my show just as professional as it can be. You can never stop learning."

Country-music fans have learned to love Tim McGraw. His long-awaited new album, *All I Want*, was released in the fall of 1995, and immediately the first single from the new endeavor, "I Like It, I Love It," raced to number one on the charts.

SAMMY KERSHAW. Sammy Kershaw—born Sammy Cashat—has a few remarkable goals left in life. Blessed with one gold and two platinum albums, the Cajun-spiced Mercury Records artist wants someday to be a member of the Grand Ole Opry, to be elected to the

"I'm going to run for governor of Louisiana one of these days," Sammy Kershaw promises the Fan Fair faithful.

Country Music Hall of Fame, and to be elected . . . governor of Louisiana?

That's right. The native of Abbeville, Louisiana, made that announcement to the fans surrounding his booth at Fan Fair '95. "I'm going to run for governor of Louisiana one of these days," Sammy told the faithful, some of whom probably ran out to register to vote.

Governor Kershaw's state dinners would probably include gumbo, crayfish étouffée, jambalaya, and pralines—all Cajun delicacies that the master chef prepares himself. This Renaissance man is not only a winner in the kitchen; he can also paint beautiful mountain landscapes, weld gates for his property near Nashville, ride up the Tennessee hills on his Harley, and go bob-bob-bobbing on his Bobcat through the woods surrounding his country home.

In 1995, Kershaw maintained a heavy touring schedule, including thirty dates with Travis Tritt. As intense as he is talented, Sammy will swear that his first greatest-hits album—*The Hits/Chapter One*—won't be his last.

You've got to believe Governor Kershaw.

JOHN MICHAEL MONTGOMERY. The Kentucky native, discovered while playing in a Lexington nightspot, has run like a Derby thoroughbred since signing on with Atlantic Records in 1992. His first single hit the top five; his next, "I Love the Way You Love Me," went all the way to number one; and in 1993, he secured his spot as one of country music's fastest-rising entertainers with his chart-topping smash "I Swear."

The handsome hunkabilly with dimples to die for wins the hearts of female fans like few other male country singers. That he's also a bachelor doesn't disappoint them a bit. His powerful voice, potent personality, and wonderful way with a song have already paved the way to three multiplatinum albums.

After opening for such acts as Reba McEntire, John Michael moved to headliner status in 1995 with his solo tour that included a gig for more than fifty thousand fans at the Houston Livestock Show and Rodeo.

"With our third album out, it was time to get out on my own," commented the driven Kentuckian, who still lives

Fan Tiffany Gill gets an autograph and a hug from the star of the John Michael Montgomery Fan Fair booth.

near Lexington. "It was time to say that I'm a grown boy, and here I am, and here is my music."

A highlight of Montgomery's year came during the Vinny Golf Tournament, hosted by Vince Gill, when the University of Kentucky fan met the team's dynamic head basketball coach, Rick Pitino. Did the meeting go well? Just ask John Michael. Pitino invited him to attend a game, sing the national anthem, and sit on the bench with the team. It doesn't get better than that for a University of Kentucky basketball fan.

A FEW MORE RISING STARS WHO HAVE ALREADY
MADE THEIR MARK

Suzy Bogguss
1992 CMA Horizon Award

Confederate Railroad
Two platinum albums: *Confederate Railroad*
and *Notorious*

Joe Diffie
First number one, in 1990, with "Home"

Tracy Lawrence
Three platinum albums: *Alibis, Sticks and Stones,*
and *I See It Now*

Patty Loveless
First number one, in 1989, with "Timber, I'm Falling in Love"

Kathy Mattea
1988 CMA Single of the Year for
"Eighteen Wheels and a Dozen Roses"

Lorrie Morgan
First number one, in 1990, with "Five Minutes"

Collin Raye
First number one, in 1991, with "Love, Me"

Sawyer Brown
First number one, in 1985, with "Step That Step"

Shenandoah
First number one, in 1989, with "The Church on
Cumberland Road"

Marty Stuart
Two Grammy Awards: Best Vocal Collaboration, 1992,
and Best Country Instrumental, 1993

Pam Tillis
1994 CMA Award for Female Vocalist of the Year

Aaron Tippin
First number one, in 1992, with
"There Ain't Nothing Wrong with the Radio"

Ricky Van Shelton
1988 CMA Horizon Award

These are the stories of just a few of the established talents making their imprint on country music as they rise to new heights. All of these acts have the talent, ability, and drive to take them right to the top of the country-music cosmos—to that impressive land of superstardom. Will they share the upper rungs of the ladder of success with such similarly gifted talents as Reba McEntire, Vince Gill, Alan Jackson, and Trisha Yearwood? Stay tuned for 1996 . . . and beyond.

Reba McEntire goes to new heights—a remote Guatemalan mountaintop village—for a stunning video shoot.

S U P E R

6 ✦

ONE NAME SAYS IT ALL

The superstars—you know them on a first-name basis:

Reba, Vince, Alan, Garth, Dwight, Trisha, Clint, Wynonna, Travis. And in a couple of cases, you know them by their first two names: Mary Chapin, Billy Ray.

Nobody needs to hear their last names to identify these stratospheric singers, who have defied gravity and became stars in their own special galaxy—a private place with daily public viewings.

S T A R S

These singers have devoted their lives to reaching the top, and they've reached it. They've reached it by spending years pursuing their dreams, by overcoming the scorn and negativity of the naysayers who line every pathway to superstardom. They have fulfilled the prophesies of those special people—family members and fans who believed in them and supported them—and thus they've fulfilled their ultimate destiny and, in most cases, found ultimate happiness.

Here's a state-of-the-art update on country's greatest reigning stars:

REBA. Her 1995 tour was something to behold. Reba McEntire, who traveled throughout the United States and Canada on more than 120 concert dates, was one of the top concert draws in America, up there with the ancient rockers and the new—the Rolling Stones, Elton John, and Pearl Jam—and ahead of every other country artist and all female artists in every genre of music.

When the Reba tour rolled into town, it provided an impressive sight: The entourage included thirteen trucks loaded with sound, lighting, and other equipment and six buses hauling the band, dancers, and singers. McEntire and her husband-manager, Narvel Blackstock, arrived on their private jet, owned by their Starstruck Jet Aviation Services Company, which owns four other planes as well.

The immense stage held Reba, Linda Davis (who also has a solo career on Arista Records), two other backup singers, an eight-piece band, and ten dancers. Behind the scenes before the ninety-minute show, eighty-four crew members would work for ten hours, setting up the stage, sound, video, lighting, and pyrotechnics—yes, the show ended with fireworks worthy of a July Fourth celebration.

Kicking off the show were such rising stars as Tracy Byrd, Rhett Akins, and Toby Keith. When Reba took the stage, she commanded it, going through more than a dozen costume changes and performing twenty-one songs. In the dazzling finale, Reba and Linda Davis performed on a platform that flew out over the audience as the dynamic duo sang their hit "Does He Love You."

Reba's 1995 travels took her beyond North America to a remote mountaintop in Guatemala, to shoot a video for her hit "And Still." The reigning Academy of Country Music Entertainer of the Year taught the village children how to sing "Old MacDonald Had a Farm" during breaks in the filming.

The tireless trouper continued to reach out to those who need help as she sponsored her second A Woman's House, a home-building venture of Habitat for Humanity, and the Reba McEntire Center for Rehabilitation.

Whether reaching out to help the less fortunate or expanding her musical adventures to new areas and arenas, Reba remains solidly in the front ranks of country music stardom.

VINCE. They don't come any better—as entertainer or as human being—than Vince Gill. He's modest beyond his means. "I'm just another guy who sings high" he tries to convey—unsuccessfully, of course. He sings high. But he's not just another guy. He's Vince Gill, and he's invincible.

His face is as sweet as his voice, and his soul is sweeter than either. He has eyes that see beyond this lifetime and a smile that could melt the polar ice caps. His talent is exceeded only by his heart—and that results in more charitable endeavors than you could shake a benefit at.

One of Vince's favorite projects is the Junior Golf program in Tennessee, which draws youngsters from all parts of the state—from inner cities to outer suburbs. More than $200,000 was raised for Junior Golf during Vince's third annual Vinny Pro-Am Golf Tournament. Held at the Golf Club of Tennessee, south of Nashville, the two-day golf- and fun-fest drew more than twenty-seven thousand fans and stars of golf and music, including Amy Grant, John Michael Montgomery, Joe Diffie, Billy Dean, Suzy Bogguss, Chet Atkins, Cleve Francis, and the 1995 British Open winner, John Daly.

Gill joined Dolly Parton for one of 1995's most surprising and successful pairings—taking Dolly's "I Will Always Love You" back up the charts for the third time. (Dolly originally took the beautiful love ballad to number one back in 1974, and Whitney Houston recorded a smash version in 1992.)

Vince Gill, father of the Vinny Golf Tournament, demonstrates how not to hold a golf club.

The duet with Dolly dueled with Vince's heartfelt tribute song to Keith Whitley and Gill's late brother,

"Go Rest High on That Mountain." While his album *When Loves Finds You* climbed the charts, Vince released a potent new album—*Souvenirs*—to power his way to 1996.

Vince continued to attract a wide variety of fans to his concerts, stretching the demographics and the generations of the country-music audience. "Some of the older folks like me because I have a gentleman's haircut, and the kids like me because I play the guitar loud and they all have a good time," Vince explained. "I'm lucky because I have a full scope of ages that come to my show."

The "just another guy who sings high" keeps going higher—and higher—and higher. And not just in vocal range.

ALAN. It was a dark and stormy night, midnight in Montgomery, a little bit spooky in the Alabama city but definitely spookier in the cemetery. The headlights of a bus pierced the fog like the beam of a lighthouse, playing over tombstones and monuments until the vehicle reached the edge of the graveyard. One by one, several men departed the bus and walked on the sodden ground as they sought the grave of a giant who died too soon.

Then Alan Jackson and his band members found it: the grave of Hank Williams. They gathered around the hallowed ground and sang Alan's ode to the man he idolizes, "Midnight in Montgomery." As their song ended, the gray sky suddenly was lit by a falling star. Then there was no music, no song. Only a soft, heartfelt, and soulful message from Alan up to where Hank just might be residing: "Thanks."

In 1995, the Arista Records artist boosted his total of platinum albums to four, having already scored with more than a dozen number-one chart-topping singles. And he has accomplished a rarity—a gold holiday album, *Honky Tonk Christmas*.

The Newnan, Georgia, native, who was inducted into the Grand Ole Opry in 1991, has enjoyed multimillion-selling success—surpassing eighteen million—on both the country album charts and the pop-music album charts. But his grandest smash could turn out to be his latest—*Alan Jackson: The Greatest Hits Collection*. They don't come bigger than this. Alan's *Hits* could easily become *the* album of 1996.

GARTH. For someone rumored to be taking the year off, Garth was a whirling dervish of activity. Our Mr. Brooks was in and out of the spotlight throughout the year, disappearing, reappearing, leaving the concert trail while planning the 1996 Garth Brooks U.S. tour, and recording a new album. He surfaced at the Academy of Country Music Awards in Los Angeles, where he won a trophy for "The Red Strokes" as best video and the Jim Reeves Memorial Award for his role in popularizing country music internationally.

What else did Garth do during his year-long "vacation"? He set up his own management firm, GB Management, directed by his brother Kelly. He formed Red Strokes Entertainment Company in Burbank—a California connection that will allow Garth to expand his range of talent into creating music for motion pictures, writing screenplays, and directing movies. And he headed back to the studio to work on a new album.

In the meantime, his first greatest-hits record created some records of its own. *The Hits* became the fastest-selling country album in history, hitting the top position in

Billboard's Pop and Country charts and surpassing the eight-million mark in sales.

Two special awards indicate Brooks's potency as an artist. The first was given to him by his record company—a multiplatinum plaque for *No Fences*. With eleven million copies, it's the biggest-selling country album of all time. The other, presented by the Recording Industry Association of America on the stage of the Grand Ole Opry, where Brooks had just performed, commemorates sales of more than ten million copies of *Ropin' the Wind*, which made history in 1991 when it became the first album to debut at number one on *Billboard*'s Pop and Country charts.

When Garth was out of the public eye this year—and that was often—he devoted quality time to his family—his wife, Sandy, and their daughters, Taylor Mayne Pearl, three years old, and August Anna, one. He also returned to the basics of writing songs for his new album, including the first single, "She's Every Woman," co-written with the singer-writer Victoria Shaw.

The Capitol Nashville Records superstar wants to take his music around the world, even to China. Influenced by such diverse talents as George Strait, George Jones, James Taylor, Elton John, Billy Joel, Kiss, and Queen, Brooks plans for his stage show to be in the same league with the major rock and pop acts. "I want to bring in the best show we've ever been able to do, demonstrating that country can be as high-tech and advanced as any other type of music," he explained.

DWIGHT. No one else in country music has more successfully created, perfected, and promoted his or her image than Dwight Yoakam. He invented attitude before it became a buzzword. He helped make frayed-at-the-knees jeans a fashion trend. The angle of his cowboy hat, the pose of his long legs, the seldom-smiling-though-alluring face—all create a powerful stage persona. Add to that the compelling honesty of his lyrics, melodies, and performance, and you've got one of the top talents in country music.

Born in Pikeville, in the eastern Kentucky hills, Dwight ended up in Los Angeles in the early eighties and meticulously plotted the course of his career. His plans never jibed with Nashville's designs for his career, so he took the southern California route, which has led to five platinum albums and a 1993 Grammy Award for Best Male Country Performance.

Dwight has emerged as one of the purest country singers since Hank Williams, George Jones, and Vern Gosdin. He reflects Waylon Jennings's answer to the question of whether Waylon could cross over to the pop-music realm: "I couldn't go pop with a mouth full of firecrackers." And neither Dwight nor Waylon cares about doing so. Like Waylon, Yoakam keeps his vision focused on what he does best—and that's making country music from the heart.

Dwight enjoyed his high-water mark with the double-platinum success of *This Time*, then released *Dwight Live* containing seventeen songs rendered live before a wildly cheering audience, and a new studio album titled *Gone*, his best yet.

There's something mysterious about this man, something remote, something reserved. It drives women crazy. But it boils down to a simple fact: Dwight Yoakam has become the Dwight Yoakam he has always wanted to be. It wasn't easy, but now he's done it—and he's only going to get bigger and better in the future.

Happily married to a Maverick, Trisha Yearwood has seen her musical philosophies evolve.

TRISHA. "I just flat-out love to sing," proclaims Trisha Yearwood. And the fans apparently flat-out love to hear her sing, for Trisha has already racked up three platinum albums and forged to the forefront as one of the leading female country singers.

Married to Robert Reynolds, bass player for the Mavericks, Trisha has seen her philosophies about love and life evolve as her album *Thinkin' About You* testified. "It was more popular than the last one because I was happily married," the MCA Records artist noted. "I could sing those songs with feeling because I realized that relationships can actually work."

Trisha was raised on a farm in Monticello, Georgia, and was influenced musically by Elvis Presley, country artists, and southern rock she heard on the radio. She moved to Nashville to enroll in the popular music-business program at Belmont University, and she learned the ropes of the Nashville music industry as an intern, then as a receptionist, at MTM Records. Trisha sang on demos for songwriters, graduated to background vocals on master sessions, and then, supported by the producer Garth Fundis, put together a showcase performance and was signed by MCA Records. Her debut single, "She's in Love with the Boy," hit number one in 1991, and her first album sold more than two million copies.

Yearwood has the power and confidence to remake other singers' songs into her own personal statements, as she does with Melissa Etheridge's "You Can Sleep While I Drive" and Tammy Wynette's " 'Til I Get It Right."

With her booming recording-and-concert-tour career in high gear, Trisha's biggest problem has been finding enough quality time to share with Robert, who has been a road warrior as well, with the red-hot Mavericks. But when either one has a break from the road, it's on to the airport. "We've got enough frequent flyer miles from flying to see each other that we should own our own plane now," quipped Trisha, with some justification.

CLINT. Born in New Jersey and raised in Houston, Clint Patrick Black added another album to his gilded collection as *One Emotion* soared beyond the half-million sales mark. Since bursting on the scene in 1989 with a string of number-one songs—"Better Man," "Killin' Time," and "Nobody's Home"—he has accumulated four platinum albums and is one of the hottest draws on the touring circuit.

Like Dwight Yoakam, Clint has taken complete control of his profession. He writes, or co-writes, most of his songs. He directs his videos. He's hands-on with all aspects of his entertainment life. "I want to be involved in anything that's creative, that relates to me," Clint emphasized. "If it's something creative, I'll work twenty hours a day and sleep four hours a night to get it done."

Those long hours also go into his drive to improve the world. He and his wife, the beautiful actress Lisa Hartman-Black, first visited Somalia in 1993, spearheading country music's fight against hunger. He made sure his Keebler Wheatables tour interfaced with USA Harvest in efforts to feed the hungry. He also joined Wynonna Judd in raising money for the victims of the Midwest floods.

The visionary Clint Black takes complete control of his career.

Singer, writer, director, humanist, Clint can now call himself an actor as well. An Opry member since 1991, Clint made his acting debut in *Maverick* and will likely pursue the avocation in the future.

WYNONNA. One of the year's most heralded returns to the stage occurred at Fan Fair '95 when Wynonna Judd came back with passion and fury after short-circuiting her 1994 concert tour to prepare for the birth of her first child, Elijah Judd Kelley.

The single-mom delivery jump-started some country music fans negatively, as Wynonna has acknowledged. Referring to some of the letters she received, Wynonna commented, "I hope they're more forgiving of their family than they are of me." While Wynonna is considering whether to marry the baby's father, Arch Kelley III, she applauds those fans who stood behind her.

The fascinating story of The Judds—Naomi and Wynonna—

Wynonna with the new love in her life, Elijah.

was broadcast as a TV miniseries, adding fuel to the mystery and meaning of the mother-daughter team from Ashland, Kentucky. The duo had fourteen number-one records and was going full-steam ahead when Naomi had to bow out in 1991 because of chronic hepatitis.

Wynonna, cast into the spotlight as a solo act, scored with three straight top-of-the-chart smashes in 1992 and has kept up the pace with her raucous blend of country, rock, gospel, and soul. Wy is not the question; Wy is the answer when it comes to red-hot country-music success in 1995 and beyond.

TRAVIS. "Country Club" propelled James Travis Tritt onto the charts at the same time Clint Black was also helping to redefine country music. The Warner Bros. Records artist soared to the top with his next release, "Help Me Hold On," and he has held on to a skyrocketing career ever since.

The major Travis Tritt gift to his fans in 1995 was the release of a generous fifteen-song album, *Greatest Hits: From the Beginning.* It was destined to join his earlier album, the wonderfully titled *Ten Feet Tall and Bulletproof,* as his fifth platinum album.

Growing up in Marietta, Georgia, Travis combined the genres that influenced him—rock, gospel, soul, and country. This powerful potpourri infuses his concerts with a synergy that even impressed veteran Waylon Jennings. "I've learned a good bit from that boy," Waylon observed. "I've learned—or relearned, I guess—that you've got to have an edge when you walk out on that stage."

Travis Tritt has that edge. And he has the staying power to be a major player in country music in the years to come.

MARY CHAPIN. As a songwriter and as a singer who dredges the depths of her soul for her wisdom and her wit, Mary Chapin Carpenter proved that she's among the best in the business. Her *Stones in the Road* album justifi-

ably became her third platinum or multiplatinum success, to go along with the one gold.

Classic chronicler of the human condition and spirit, Mary Chapin Carpenter.

Chapin, as her friends know her, has put a lock on the Grammy Award for Best Female Country Vocal Performance, winning the coveted honor for the past four years. The Columbia Records artist can go from soft to harsh, vulnerable to victorious, and quiet to loud in one fell swoop, depending on what she's singing. Those compositions range from the in-your-face "Shut Up and Kiss Me" to one of the most devastatingly emotional songs of lost love closing one of life's chapters, "The End of My Pirate Days."

As she described her latest album, Mary Chapin, who has gone from the folk scene to modern country, acknowledged that her world vision has taken a different turn. "It's not so much about changing the world, but how your world changes." There's not an artist on earth who surpasses Mary Chapin in ability to chronicle those sometimes subtle, sometimes dramatic changes in one's shifting world.

BILLY RAY. In 1992, he burst into show-business mega-success with an "Achy Breaky Heart" and the biggest-selling debut album in history, *Some Gave All*, which soared into the ten-million sales region. Despite the breakthrough, Billy Ray Cyrus was not an overnight sensation. He played the hard-to-play clubs and the smoky honky-tonks for as long as, or longer than, many of those who have never been tagged with the overnight-success label.

The Flatwoods, Kentucky, native continued to hone and refine his career with the gilded status of his latest Mercury Records/Nashville album, *Storm in the Heartland*, which joined platinum platters *Some Gave All* and *It Won't Be the Last*. "My focus is on my music, what I'm doing now and in the future . . . " he told *Country Weekly* reporter Shannon Parks. "The music will stand for itself. . . . All you've got to do is search the music to find my soul."

Billy Ray's soul is never more evident than in his contributions to charity, sometimes as a headliner and often behind the scenes, as when he flew a tiny preteen AIDS victim to Nashville for a performance and backstage visit, complete with hugs and kisses. Billy Ray also gained a mustache—a white one—when he became the first male star to be featured in the popular "Milk Mustache" advertisements sponsored by the American Heart Association and the Milk Council. Back in eastern Kentucky, neighbors take care of one another—and that's the message the gifted writer-singer has been taking to the masses.

These superstars have worked hard to get where they are. Though their backgrounds are diverse, they are joined at the hip by incredible God-given talent, a focus and drive that propel them through all the hurdles and pitfalls of this competitive battlefield, and a sense of humanity that makes them want to give so much back to their fans and to the less fortunate people on planet Earth.

These creators are still striving. For what? For that *next* realm. The last earthly stratum of country-music success—the sacred land populated by the likes of Johnny Cash, Willie Nelson, Dolly Parton, Merle Haggard, Loretta Lynn, George Jones, and Tammy Wynette. The top of the country-music cosmos is held for those who have been inducted into the hallowed Country Music Hall of Fame, or will be someday soon.

QUOTABLE QUOTES FROM 1995

"The reason country music is so popular right now is because it kind of reminds me of the rock and roll music I used to listen to. . . . What we considered to be hard rock then is country music now."
—*Reba McEntire, at an October 1, 1995, press conference*

" 'Go Rest High on That Mountain' was started after Keith Whitley died but I didn't finish it and stuck it away in a drawer and it stayed there for years. After I lost my brother, I opened that drawer, realized that this has to be it and finished it."
—*Vince Gill, in an interview with Gerry Wood, July 11, 1995*

"I've always told my wife, Denise, 'You're about the only one that I can really trust to tell me the truth. You've got to keep me in line.' So she does."
—*Alan Jackson, in an interview with Bruce Honick,* Country Weekly, *October 31, 1995*

"I had a fan tell me, 'I know you're going to disappear for a while, but take your time because we'll be there when you come back.' Please tell the fans not to give up on us because we're going to be there for them."
—*Garth Brooks, in an interview with Gerry Wood, January 7, 1995*

"Cole is my black Labrador. Any time I have a dog around, it's a better day."
—*Clint Black, in an interview with Robyn Flans,* Country Weekly, *August 1, 1995*

"The late-night convenience-store stop has become a ritual. . . . Mission: Find the most disgusting and/or ridiculous gimcracks, whatchamacallits, thingamajigs for group discussion and replenish your stocks of Sunchips, smokes, microwave mystery dinners, chocolate Yoo-Hoos and Gummy Bears."
—*Mary Chapin Carpenter,* Stones in the Road Tour Book, *1995*

VETERANS

Together again:
the magical musical
reunion of George Jones
and Tammy Wynette.

7

FROM BLUE HIGHWAYS TO THE COUNTRY MUSIC HALL OF FAME

Some came from tiny towns you've never heard of, strangers to a strange land. Before the interstates became the main roads into Nashville, they took the blue highways, like routes 41, 70, and 31W. Others—before Amtrak shut down the Chicago-Miami *Floridian*—arrived at Nashville's grand Union Station.

The moderate-sized mecca of Music City didn't exactly welcome them with open arms. They had to fight, scratch, and sometimes crawl to get where they are today.

They are the country-music icons who have been inducted into the Country Music Hall of Fame—or who will be one day soon. George Jones, Tammy Wynette, Merle Haggard, Loretta Lynn, Charley Pride, Waylon Jennings, Willie Nelson, Johnny Cash, Kris Kristofferson, Emmylou Harris, Dolly Parton, George Strait, and Tanya Tucker—thirteen country-music giants who have earned what few humans on earth receive—immortality.

Where are they now? Resting on their well-earned laurels? Leading a shy and retiring life? Coasting on their millions? Getting off the exhausting concert trail? Forget it. These tremendous talents are farther into the mainstream of country-music activity than they've ever been. And they're enjoying it more than ever before.

GEORGE JONES AND TAMMY WYNETTE. These names will be inextricably linked in the annals of country music. Both performers have had sensational solo careers (George was elected to the Country Music Hall of Fame in 1992). Both have served as role models for scores of the new breed of country singers. Both have had major health problems, especially in the last few years. They loved each other at one time and were married at one time. They hated each other at another time and broke up. And the good news is that George and Tammy are happily married—but not to each other—and now get along great both onstage and off.

After more than fifteen years adrift as a duo, the country dream team returned in 1995 with a memorable album entitled *One*, a video, and a show that became one of the hottest country concert attractions of the year.

"It was like we never quit," said Tammy. "It was just wonderful getting back and singing again."

Observed George, "It takes time to heal things, and they've been healed quite a while between us."

Though country radio largely continues to ignore the acts that made country music great, like George and Tammy, the reunited duo was one of the biggest hits of 1995.

MERLE HAGGARD. How many of country music's superstars, neostars, and wanna-be stars have been influenced by Merle Haggard? The simple answer is—most of them. Like Hank Williams and George Jones, this man is music to the core. Just ask George Strait, whose all-time favorite country song is Haggard's classic "Okie from Muskogee."

Merle's childhood and rough-and-rowdy early adulthood were troubled. He escaped a traumatic youth in Bakersfield, California, where he served time at San Quentin from 1957 to 1960, before the age of twenty-one. California's governor Ronald Reagan later granted him a full pardon.

Influenced by such immortals as Bob Wills, Lefty Frizzell, and Jimmie Rodgers, the Hag eventually joined their ranks with an incredible career that has included nearly forty number-one records and a solid ten years of only top-ten songs. He and his Bakersfield buddy Buck Owens, another potential Hall of Famer, helped popularize the Bakersfield sound—a no-frills, down-home style that put a refreshing spin on country music in the 1960s and '70s.

Merle, also one of country music's best writers, can easily vamp from the knee-jerk reactionism of "The Fightin' Side of Me" to the sensuous tenderness of the heartbreaking ballad "If We Make It Through December." He was welcomed as a member of the Country Music Hall of Fame in 1994.

LORETTA LYNN. It was a tough year for Loretta Lynn. The Country Music Hall of Fame inductee spent most of her time off the road and out of sight, caring for her husband, Mooney, who battled severe health problems.

Born in Butcher Hollow, Kentucky, Loretta comes from

creative stock that spawned such singers as her brother Jay Lee Webb, her sisters Crystal Gayle (born Brenda Gail Webb) and Peggy Sue Webb, and her distant cousin Patty Loveless. Loretta's poverty-to-victory life story

Loretta Lynn rarely made public appearances in 1995 so she could care for her ailing husband, Mooney.

is the theme of her signature song, her autobiography, and a movie, all bearing the title "Coal Miner's Daughter," which are three of the best works to chronicle the life and times of a country-music star.

Loretta's first chart record was the 1960 hit "I'm a Honky Tonk Girl," on Zero Records. Her first number-one hit arrived six years later, the memorable "Don't Come Home a-Drinkin' (with Lovin' on Your Mind)," on Decca, one of the first songs in country-music history in which a woman stood up to a man with an in-your-face threat.

Her duets with Conway Twitty are legendary. The duo's first five records, starting with "After the Fire Is Gone," reached number one, and all twelve ended up in the top ten, a remarkable achievement.

Famous for her renditions of such songs as Shel Silverstein's "One's on the Way," Loretta Lynn is also known for her direct and forceful songwriting. Her producer, the legendary Owen Bradley, noted, "I told Loretta one time that I thought she was like a female Hank Williams even though she wrote things that were completely different." Loretta, who joined the Grand Ole Opry in 1962, was elected to the Country Music Hall of Fame in 1988, following Owen Bradley's induction by fourteen years.

CHARLEY PRIDE. Though Charley Pride wasn't the first black musician to make an impact on country music—African-Americans from DeFord Bailey to Ray Charles have added to the richness and depth of the genre—he has been the most important.

Pride has proved that country music is open not only to new styles but to old traditions, not only to hillbillies from eastern Kentucky but to black-skinned talents from Mississippi. This shoo-in for the Country Music Hall of Fame received the CMA's ultimate accolade, Entertainer of the Year, in 1971.

"No one had ever told me that whites were supposed to sing one kind of music and blacks another," Pride

Former baseball star Charley Pride has a ball outside his Branson theater.

asserted in his autobiography *Pride: The Charley Pride Story.* "I sang what I liked in the only voice I had."

A member of the Grand Ole Opry, Pride has recorded thirteen gold albums and has won three Grammy Awards. His early field of dreams included baseball, where he became a hitting and pitching star in the former Negro American League and Pioneer League. But he left ball for ballads after being discovered by Red Sovine in 1963.

Pride ended up, three years later, with RCA, where he recorded under the name Country Charley Pride. Emphasis on the *Country*, please. No publicity photos were released. No mention of race, creed, or color in the biographies. Just a voice for the masses to judge.

They judged, and they loved. Pride's first three songs reached the top ten. Then, when Charley appeared on stage to sing his songs, the predominantly white audiences noticed something different: He was black. They didn't care.

Pride's career zoomed. "All I Have to Offer You (Is Me)" ignited a string of number ones in 1969, and the chart hits carried Charley through 1989. Today Pride fans can catch their man in action at the Charley Pride Theater in Branson, Missouri.

WILLIE NELSON. There is no stronger heart, no better soul in country music than Willie's. There is also no one else like him, and there never will be. This man is an American Original.

His friend Kris Kristofferson summed it up best. When Willie was honored with the Academy of Country Music's Pioneer Award in 1992, Kris, emceeing the tribute, called Nelson "a carved-in-granite samurai poet warrior Gypsy guitar-pickin' wild man with a heart as big as Texas and the greatest sense of humor in the West." In 1993, when Willie was inducted into the Country Music Hall of Fame, Kris spoke eloquently again: "Willie Nelson's artistry has carried country music to a level of acceptance that it has never known. Uncompromisingly true to himself, he has fashioned a body of work that is traditional and absolutely original, appealing to rockers and farmers and bikers and lawyers—white collar, blue collar, no collar."

The Abbott, Texas, native is now clear with the IRS, following a fourteen-year debt of some seventeen million dollars that has finally been settled. A classic songwriter— "Crazy" for Patsy Cline, "Funny How Time Slips Away" for Billy Walker, and "Night Life" for Ray Price—Willie is also known for his eclectic duet partners: Merle Haggard, Julio Iglesias, Tracy Nelson, Hank Cochran, Leon Russell, Ray Price, Roger Miller, Webb Pierce, Dolly Parton, Brenda Lee, Ray Charles, and David Allan Coe.

Willie's best-known partner is his buddy Waylon Jennings. The two scored with three number-one

Willie Nelson helps raise another million dollars for small-farm families at Farm Aid in Louisville.

hits, including the multimillion-selling "Mammas Don't Let Your Babies Grow Up to Be Cowboys." This year saw the return to the road of the fearless foursome, the Highwaymen—Willie, Waylon, Kris, and Johnny Cash.

Willie, who has won the CMA's Entertainer of the Year Award and has hosted his legendary July Fourth Picnic concerts in Texas, is probably proudest of his role as president of Farm Aid, a continuing benefit for financially whipped farmers throughout the country. This year's Farm Aid drew some 47,500 fans to Cardinal Stadium in Louisville, Kentucky, for a sold-out seven-hour concert featuring Willie, John Conlee, Steve Earle, BlackHawk, Radney Foster, and such potent noncountry acts as Hootie & the Blowfish, Neil Young, and John Mellencamp. The concert raised more than one million dollars for the beleaguered small farmers of America.

JOHNNY CASH. No two words better sum up the best in country music than the name of this giant, the Man in Black. Even bank ATM machines have been named Johnny Cash. On a sun-splashed summer day in 1995, Cash's son, John Carter Cash, married the beautiful Mary Ann Joska. And on that day, the Man in Black wore white, leading Waylon Jennings to proclaim, "Damn, Johnny looks good! He's been wearing the wrong color all these years."

The Arkansas native rose to fame on Sam Phillips's legendary Sun Records in Memphis. The Johnny Cash breakthrough record was the 1956 smash "I Walk the Line," one of the multitude of hits Cash would enjoy during one of the most illustrious careers in country and pop music.

Cash played the *Louisiana Hayride* and the Grand Ole Opry and from 1969 to 1971 hosted his own ABC-TV show, taped in Nashville's Ryman Auditorium. In 1968, Cash married June Carter of the famed Carter Family after work- ing with her on the road for seven years.

Now the Cash family has grown rich in musical talent. Johnny and June's son is a musician, and their

Johnny Cash, the Man in Black, shows off his white ensemble for his son's wedding.

daughter, Rosanne, and June's stepdaughter, Carlene (whose father is the country singer Carl Smith), have achieved chart success with their styles that swerve between country and rock.

A member of the Rock and Roll Hall of Fame, Johnny Cash has won the top CMA awards, including 1969's Entertainer of the Year, and the Grammy Living Legend Award. He was elected to the Country Music Hall of Fame in 1980.

Cash still maintains an active recording and touring career, including one of the stints he likes best—as part of the superstar foursome, the Highwaymen.

WAYLON AND KRIS. Jennings and Kristofferson. Two more sure-shot entries into Country Music's Hall of Fame. Ready. Aim. Fire these guys into the bull's-eye of country's most prestigious address on Music Row, Nashville, Tennessee.

Born in Texas, Waylon worked in radio as a deejay and played bass for the late and great Buddy Holly. Yes, it's true he gave up his seat on the ill-fated plane flight that day, the one Don McLean musically described as "the day the music died."

Buddy's music died in that crash, but Waylon moved on. One of the leaders of the energizing outlaw movement of country music, which included such escape artists as Willie, Kris, and Tompall Glaser, Waylon won the CMA's Male Vocalist honors in 1975. He is married to the beautiful country singer Jessi Colter, whose captivating "I'm Not Lisa" carried her to the top of the country charts in 1975. His powerful persona and true-to-the-core creative focus will leave an indelible imprint in the ranks of country greats.

What do you say about Waylon's buddy Kris Kristofferson? Swashbucklingly handsome, wise beyond his years, a damn good actor, and a singer, Kris helped bridge the Nashville of old—Faron Young, Roger Miller, Webb Pierce—and the Nashville of new.

Somewhere in the ranks of all-time great writers—up there with Hank Williams, Harlan Howard, Don Gibson, and Dolly Parton—you've got to make room for the man who took songwriting to a new stratosphere. "Me and Bobby McGee," "Help Me Make It Through the Night," "For the Good Times," and "Why Me" are simply some of the best songs ever written.

A native of Brownsville, Texas, former Rhodes scholar, former helicopter pilot, consummate actor, former husband of mega-talent Rita Coolidge, father of many children, and friend of all who need a friend, Kris Kristofferson epitomizes what country music could be, is, and will be.

EMMYLOU HARRIS. This beauty from Birmingham, Alabama, worked as a folk singer in the Washington, D.C., area and toured with the Flying

Emmylou Harris and Trisha Yearwood merge their talents during a benefit performance for the Second Harvest Food Bank.

Burrito Brothers and the legendary Gram Parsons. Her songs are as wistful as the wind through the willows, her voice as pure as a mountain stream, and her soul as deep as the center of the cosmos. The future Hall of Fame will not be worthy of its name without the inclusion of this sensuous, talent-laden beauty who has been churning out country hits for twenty years.

Rather than rest on her laurels, in 1995 Emmylou went into Nashville's Woodland Studios and New Orleans's Kingsway Studio to record one of her most innovative and powerful albums. The title track, "Wrecking Ball," and the song "Deeper Well" are worth the price of this collection; her version of Steve Earle's masterpiece "Goodbye" elevates this album to the best-ever ranks.

Make a place for Emmy, please. Maybe between Hank and Merle, OK?

DOLLY PARTON. The mega-talented beauty from the mountains of East Tennessee spent a busy year expanding her country-music empire. The energetic and delightful Dolly covered all bases—from music to merchandising—with style, zest, and creativity.

Dolly's new album, *Something Special,* climbed toward the top of the charts while her duet with Vince Gill, "I Will Always Love You," raced up the singles chart. The evergreen song, written by Dolly, had previously hit number one three times—first by Dolly back in 1974, then a new version from Dolly's movie *The Best Little Whorehouse in Texas* in 1982, and it reached the top of the pop charts in 1992 thanks to Whitney Houston's beautiful version for the movie *The Bodyguard.*

Following the success of her bestselling autobiography *Dolly: My Life and Other Unfinished Business,* Parton now

Dolly Parton and Vince Gill share a duet on Dolly's "I Will Always Love You," a highlight of the CMA Awards show.

plans a sequel. Dolly also began work on her second children's book, which follows *Coat of Many Colors*.

Dolly's own theme park, Dollywood, in Pigeon Forge, Tennessee, continues to grow in popularity and size. An eight-million-dollar project on Dollywood Boulevard, a tribute to movie-star glamour, opens in 1996. The Dollywood Foundation has become an important charitable organization for East Tennessee youngsters, providing medical services and scholarships.

Another venture, the Dixie Stampede dining and entertainment arena, opened in Branson, Missouri. It's Dolly's third Dixie Stampede—an unusual attraction that spotlights entertainers on horseback.

From a new line of lingerie to food to beauty products, Dolly has become a master of mass-marketing frenzy. When does the woman sleep? Perhaps never: Dolly reveals that her most productive hours are from three A.M. to seven A.M.

OK, so the next singers are not grizzled veterans like some of the other subjects of this chapter. They look, act, and sing young, but they are veterans who have dominated the hearts and charts of the country-music world for years—in George Strait's case for fifteen years, and in Tanya Tucker's, for an amazing twenty-three. The doors of the Country Music Hall of Fame will some day swing open for these gifted performers.

GEORGE STRAIT. Fans of George Strait eagerly awaited September 12, 1995, the day MCA Records released the four-disc boxed set titled *Strait Out of the Box*. The George collection is packed with seventy-two songs—from new ballads to past hits. He had a lot of material

George continues his ride "Strait" to the top.

to choose from: the pride of Poteet, Texas, has amassed thirty-one number-one songs and eight gold and eleven platinum albums.

Although Strait has reached the top of his profession, he'd like to reach the top of another profession—team roping. Once again this year he staged the George Strait Team Roping Classic in Kingsville, Texas, which drew the top professional ropers in the country. George made it into the second round of the rodeo event but failed to make the finals of his own tournament. "Wait till next year" became the instant theme of the 1996 version of the activity George likes best.

Although George loves the thrill of performing and receiving applause and acclaim from his fans, the handsome cowboy is most at home on his ranch in the South Texas brush country between Laredo and San Antonio. Home on the range is where George continues to pursue his favorite activities—raising animals, fishing, and of course, roping. He seldom approaches a guitar when he's at home.

His love of animals prompted him to market pet products. Got horses? Try Strait Country natural-scented or apple-scented shampoo and conditioner for horses. Got dogs? Go straight to George for Strait Nutrition liver treats for dogs.

Pet food or platinum, George Strait has it all. And the country fans keep buying whatever he happens to be selling.

TANYA TUCKER. Whether she walks into a small room or a fifty-thousand-seat arena, Tanya Tucker exudes enough energy, verve, drive, and raw sexuality to run the thermometers up an extra twenty degrees. Born October 10, 1958, in Seminole, Texas, Tanya was only thirteen when she enjoyed her first chart record—"Delta Dawn"—which hit number six on *Billboard*'s country listing in 1972.

Ten number ones, seven gold albums, and four platinum albums later, Tanya continues to light up the charts and the concert trail. Capitol Nashville Records released a fifty-eight-song boxed set of four CDs, and her album sales have now surpassed the seven-million mark.

Tucker's show-business life has several different facets. She's one of the queens of benefits, appearing at numerous fund-raising affairs throughout the country, including Country in the Rockies, a Crested Butte, Colorado, event benefiting the Frances Williams Preston Research Laboratories, a division of the T. J. Martell Foundation for leukemia, cancer, and AIDS research. Tanya's business ventures include her Tanya Tucker Collection, a line of western wear, and her super-spicy salsa, which lives up to its namesake.

Whether it's business, pleasure, or pleasing audiences, Tanya does it with the flair, ability, and electricity that will one day land her in the Country Music Hall of Fame.

Whom have we left out? Ronnie Milsap might make it beyond these hallowed borders. John Anderson's career died on the vine and then came powerfully back to life. Anne Murray, the Canadian chanteuse, deserves a shot. As do supergroup Alabama, Tom T. Hall, the Judds, Sonny James, Brenda Lee, Jerry Lee Lewis, Mel Tillis, Conway Twitty, and Faron Young.

Let's enter a plea here for the Country Music Association to induct more than one artist per year into the Hall of Fame. This will allow some of yesterday's and today's top talents into the venerable hall before they're long gone, uplifted into hillbilly heaven. Let them enjoy the strong, if only brief, camaraderie with this august body of country music's all-time greats.

COUNTRY MUSIC'S FAMILY TREE
The Who's Who of Who's Sung with Whom

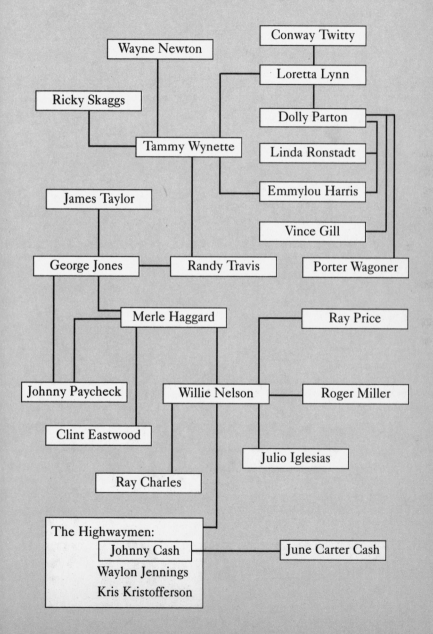

Opry members react in a variety of ways as the seventieth-anniversary birthday cake erupts into fireworks.

SEVENTY YEARS

8

THE GRANDEST OLE OPRY

"I don't know if Nashville or country music would exist if it wasn't for the foundation supplied by the Grand Ole Opry." Did this profound and powerful comment come from one of the Opry's old-time greats—Bill Monroe, Little Jimmy Dickens, or Porter Wagoner? No, it came from the Country Music Association's 1995 Entertainer of the Year, Alan Jackson. The Opry member—class of 1991—went on to say, "If it wasn't for the Opry, some of the younger traditional country-music singers would not have learned the style or been inspired to sing it." Alan was talking about himself and other traditionally oriented young acts.

Born as the WSM Barn Dance on November 28, 1925, the world's longest-running radio show celebrated its seventieth anniversary in 1995. Three years after its launch over the saturating fifty-thousand-watt Nashville station, the show received the name that stuck. It happened when DeFord Bailey, the African-American Harmonica Wizard, finished a rip-roaring version of "Pan American Blues." The Opry's broadcasting founder, George D. Hay, who dubbed himself "The Solemn Old Judge," noted that the show had followed an NBC radio presentation of classical music. He announced, "For the past hour we have been listening to music taken largely from Grand Opera, but from now on we will present the Grand Ole Opry!"

The first home for the Opry was a tiny radio studio in the National Life and Accident Insurance Company building. National Life, which owned WSM, soon had to move the show to larger quarters, for fans started flocking to the shows. Studio A led to Studio B; then the five-hundred-seat Studio C was constructed. In the 1930s, as the show's fame spread and the audiences grew, the Opry moved to the Hillsboro Theater, from there to the Dixie Tabernacle, to the War Memorial Auditorium, and in 1943 to the Ryman Auditorium, which came to be known as the Mother Church of Country Music. In 1974, the Opry left the Ryman for Opryland USA. (The historic Ryman Auditorium, once slated to become yet another downtown Nashville parking lot, was saved, beautifully restored, and since 1994 has been alive with the sounds of music from country to pop.)

Now located in the four-thousand-seat state-of-the-art Grand Ole Opry House at Opryland USA, the Grand Ole Opry still beams its broadcasts over WSM radio while a half-hour Saturday-night Opry segment is televised over TNN: The Nashville Network. Two shows are staged on Saturday nights and one on Friday nights, except from May 1 to October 31, when the Opry presents two Friday shows. During each performance, the fans never know who will appear on the hallowed stage. NO TELLING WHO'LL SURPRISE YOU AT THE OPRY, the advertisements and billboards proclaim.

Despite its seventy years, the Opry manages to stay, in the words of the Bob Dylan song, "forever young." "The evolution, the evolvement of the show is why it's seventy years old," observed Bob Whittaker, vice president and general manager of the Opry and Opryland Productions. "There was a time when people were wondering how long will Bill Monroe and Hank Snow and Little Jimmy Dickens be able to keep this thing going? And all of a sudden here comes a Porter Wagoner on it and here comes a Bill Anderson on it. This has happened throughout the years."

The Grand Ole Opry, seventy years young. And the new generation joined its elders in appreciation of this, the most venerable of venues. "No matter how long or how far my career goes, my Grand Ole Opry membership is among the class of honors that will never be topped for me," praised Garth Brooks.

Whittaker expects the evolution to continue with today's new breed of performers, many of them throwbacks to the traditional greats who made the Opry what it is. "This is what's going to happen with the Garth Brookses, the Alan Jacksons, the Clint Blacks, and the

Alison Krausses of the world. They love coming to the Opry. People who are the superstars of today will be the legends of ten and fifteen years from now."

Opry memories are some of the most vivid slice-of-life sequences in the history of country music: Roy Acuff giving his legendary performances of "The Great Speckled Bird" starting in 1938; Hank Williams wailing his heartfelt, soul-searching songs in his 1949 debut, which won six encores; Bob Wills and Elvis Presley confounding Opry leaders and audiences with their individualistic styles and personas; the soul star James Brown, an Opry fan, making a controversial appearance in 1979 following an introduction by Porter Wagoner, a Brown fan; and the ever-wonderful, ever-witty, ever-loving Minnie Pearl, whose health unfortunately kept her from appearing at the Opry in 1995.

Every year great Opry memories are made, and 1995 was no exception. This year was in fact presidential. Former president George Bush and his wife, former first lady Barbara Bush, celebrated their fiftieth wedding anniversary with a special tribute performance by their Opry and country-music friends at the Opry House. The Oak Ridge Boys hosted the event, titled With Love, from Nashville—A Celebration of the Fiftieth Anniversary of George and Barbara Bush. After enjoying such stars as Lorrie Morgan, Loretta Lynn, Vince Gill, and Amy Grant, the former chief executive commented, "It was an emotional, wonderful night. If you knew how happy all of these people have made us. Thank you so very much for a special evening we'll never forget."

It was also the year the Opry gained a mascot—a droopy-eyed hound dog, named Ole Blu, hailing from a family of plush animal characters from Mighty Star Toymakers.

Not all of the Opry's 1995 highlights took place onstage. A Porter Wagoner roast at the Opryland Hotel brought one-time partners/one-time foes Porter Wagoner and Dolly Parton back together in a big way. Barbs, jokes, and warm, tender accolades marked the February 26 fund-raising event, with proceeds going to the Dan Ruby Cancer Center at Nashville's St. Thomas Hospital.

Dolly Parton barb: "I thought it took a lot of nerve for

Flanked by Oak Ridge Boys Steve Sanders, Richard Sterban, Duane Allen, and Joe Bonsall, former president George Bush and Barbara Bush celebrate their fiftieth anniversary at the Opry House.

Porter to ask me to come to the roast. But I knew he had nerve when he sued me for a million dollars when he was only paying me a hundred dollars a week."

Dolly barb, part two: "One time Jeannie Seely and Tammy Wynette came to me real concerned because of a rumor going around that Porter was saying he had slept with us. They wondered what we should do. I said, 'Don't worry about this, girls, because half of the people will think Porter's lying and the other half will think we've got bad taste.'"

Chet Atkins barb: "They had a tornado out there in Porter's hometown of West Plains, Missouri, and it did one hundred thousand dollars' worth of improvements."

Ralph Emery barb: "I remember when Porter's hair was dark and Hank Snow's hair was real."

Perspective from E. W. "Bud" Wendell, president and chief executive officer of Gaylord Entertainment, which owns the Opry: "Porter is one of the greatest all-around entertainers in country music. He has been a stabilizing influence on the country music mainstream for three decades and is one of the best-loved members of the Grand Ole Opry."

Porter's reply: "I've been blessed with the love that all of you have shared with me throughout my life. And

Porter Wagoner tries in vain to counter some of Dolly Parton's hilarious barbs during the Porter Wagoner Roast.

Dolly, you're a very, very special person and I love you very much."

It doesn't get better than this. But at the Opry, it does get as good. "Another magical, special night this year was when I had Ray Price booked on the show," recalled Whittaker. "Willie Nelson was over at an Opryland theater, so I called Willie's people and asked what was the chance for Willie to do a walk-on with Ray at the Opry. A few minutes later, I got a call back that said, 'Very good, if Ray will come over here and do a walk-on with Willie.' " Two walk-ons later Opryland and Opry fans were in their own nirvana. "It was really magic at the Grand Ole Opry when Willie Nelson, unannounced, walked onstage after Ray Price started singing 'San Antonio Rose.' "

Two weeks later Mickey Gilley and Jerry Lee Lewis walked out onstage together, totally surprising the audience again. Reports Whittaker, "The audience went bananas with Jerry Lee on the piano and Mickey singing. They had to do an encore."

The CMA's Entertainer of the Year, Alan Jackson, is a hard act to refuse, even when he calls in at the last second. "We got a call from Alan from his plane, and he said he should hit the ground by eleven-thirty and 'I think I can be at the Opry by twenty till. Can I do a walk-on?' Here comes Alan Jackson in, and no one in the audience expects to see him. He does four numbers for us. These are the great moments."

Some of the Opry's 1995 shows were slanted to various themes: On February 4, the hallowed halls roared with comedy from Johnny Russell, Grandpa Jones, Chonda Pierce, and Jerry Clower. Artists Connie Smith, the Crossman Quartet, J. D. Sumner and the Stamps, and the 4 Guys uplifted the audience with gospel on May 27.

Pure sounds of bluegrass took over on August 19, with Mike Snider, Claire Lynch, the Nashville Bluegrass Band, and the Osborne Brothers. The Grand Ladies of the Opry—Jean Shepard, Jeannie Seely, Skeeter Davis, and Jan Howard—had their night to shine on September 23.

It's true: No one can ever predict who will show up at the Opry, and this year Opry fans carried away many memorable moments, including the appearance of two Country Music Hall of Famers—George Jones and Chet Atkins—on the July 1 show; on August 26, Dolly Parton, Porter Wagoner, and a surprise appearance by Vince Gill, who sang a duet with Dolly; and on September 9, Country Music Hall of Fame member and former Louisiana governor Jimmie Davis—a vibrant ninety-three years young—who performed his famous song "You Are My Sunshine." Rest assured there will be many more nights of this cosmic country-music mélange in the future.

These were all great moments at the Opry in 1995—the year that two diverse talents—Bashful Brother Oswald and Martina McBride—fulfilled their lifelong dreams to become members of the most famous show on earth. And it was in 1995 that the Opry celebrated its seventieth anniversary. On October 2, Porter Wagoner initiated the celebrations by ringing the opening bell at the New York Stock Exchange to commemorate the anniversary. The special birthday party, held at the Opry House on October 13 and 14, was made even more special by the show's oldest continuing sponsor, Martha White Foods, which is perhaps the longest-reigning sponsor in advertising history, going back to 1948. The 16,000 Opry attendees received cupcakes courtesy of Martha White and music courtesy of such acts as Little Jimmy Dickens, John Conlee, Jeanne Pruett, Porter Wagoner, Del Reeves, Bill Carlisle, and Martina McBride. As a fitting tribute, the Opry staffers rolled a giant birthday cake onstage while the cast sang an appropriate "Happy Birthday" to the world's longest-running radio show. As they sang, fireworks erupted from the cake.

Bob Whittaker proclaimed, "We're celebrating seventy years of music and magic at the Grand Ole Opry, and we wanted to make the occasion

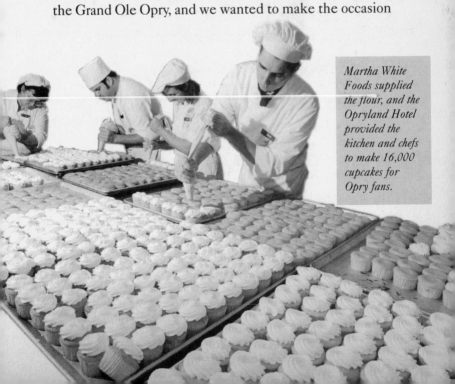

Martha White Foods supplied the flour, and the Opryland Hotel provided the kitchen and chefs to make 16,000 cupcakes for Opry fans.

Welcome To
THE GRAND OLE OPRY FAMILY
BASHFUL BROTHER OSWALD
Jan. 21, 1995

special for those fans who attend our shows during this birthday weekend." Some 16,000 cupcakes later, the Opry fans went home full from music and food.

Other events celebrating the anniversary included a Bluegrass Spectacular featuring the Father of Bluegrass, Bill Monroe, at the Opry House and performances of the musical *Always . . . Patsy Cline* at the Ryman Auditorium.

The seventieth anniversary of the Opry earned a two-hour CBS-TV special, taped November 30, which included the induction of the Opry's newest member,

Still bashful after all these years, Bashful Brother Oswald receives congratulations for his Opry induction from Grandpa Jones and John Hartford.

Martina McBride. Among those taking part in the televised festivities were Dolly Parton, Vince Gill, and Alan Jackson. Great moments for the great Grand Ole Opry.

Those wanting to attend 1996 performances can call (615) 889-6611 for specific dates and times.

Remarkably, the Grand Ole Opry, the radio show that resulted in Nashville's being named Music City, USA, remains as fresh and original as its first broadcast, which showcased the eighty-year-old fiddler Uncle Jimmy Thompson sitting in a chair before a vintage microphone. Now the greatest talents of the past merge their remarkable skills with the new standouts, who will populate the future of country music to form—the Grand Ole Brand New Opry.

Minnie Pearl, the jewel of the Opry's past, described the ambience best when she remembered the wise words of the "Solemn Old Judge," George D. Hay, who helped

> To join the Grand Ole Opry Fan Club, write to: Grand Ole Opry Fan Club 2804 Opryland Drive Nashville, TN 37214
>
> Dues are $10 annually

young Minnie conquer her stage fright before her first Opry performance. "Just love 'em, honey, and they'll love you right back."

That advice worked for Minnie—and for all the Opry acts who followed her. And it still works magic today. The Opry performers just love the audience—and the audience loves them right back.

★ CURRENT GRAND

(Date signifies year inducted)

* Bill Monroe *(1939)*
* Minnie Pearl *(1940)*
* Grandpa Jones *(1947)*
* Little Jimmy Dickens *(1948)*
* Hank Snow *(1950)*
* Teddy Wilburn *(1953)*
* Bill Carlisle *(1953)*
* Justin Tubb *(1955)*
* Jean Shepard *(1955)*
* Charlie Louvin *(1955)*
* Jimmy C. Newman *(1956)*
* Wilma Lee Cooper *(1957)*
* Porter Wagoner *(1957)*
* Roy Drusky *(1958)*
* Don Gibson *(1958)*
* Billy Grammer *(1959)*
* Skeeter Davis *(1959)*
* Billy Walker *(1960)*
* George Hamilton IV *(1960)*
* Charlie Walker *(1960)*
* Hank Locklin *(1960)*
* Bill Anderson *(1961)*
* Loretta Lynn *(1962)*
* Jim Ed Brown *(1963)*
* Jim & Jesse *(1964)*
* Ernie Ashworth *(1964)*
* The Osborne Brothers *(1964)*
* Ray Pillow *(1966)*
* Del Reeves *(1966)*
* Stu Phillips *(1967)*
* Jeannie Seely *(1967)*
* Jack Greene *(1967)*
* The 4 Guys *(1967)*
* Stonewall Jackson *(1969)*
* George Jones *(1969)*
* Dolly Parton *(1969)*

OLE OPRY CAST ★ ★

★ Jan Howard *(1971)*
★ Connie Smith *(1971)*
★ Barbara Mandrell *(1972)*
★ Jeanne Pruett *(1973)*
★ Jerry Clower *(1973)*
★ Ronnie Milsap *(1976)*
★ Larry, Steve, and Rudy—the Gatlins *(1976)*
★ Tom T. Hall *(1980)*
★ The Melvin Sloan Dancers *(1980)*
★ Boxcar Willie *(1981)*
★ John Conlee *(1981)*
★ Ricky Skaggs *(1982)*
★ Riders in the Sky *(1982)*
★ The Whites *(1984)*
★ Lorrie Morgan *(1984)*
★ Johnny Russell *(1985)*
★ Reba McEntire *(1986)*
★ Mel McDaniel *(1986)*
★ Randy Travis *(1986)*
★ Roy Clark *(1987)*
★ Ricky Van Shelton *(1988)*
★ Holly Dunn *(1989)*
★ Mike Snider *(1990)*
★ Garth Brooks *(1990)*
★ Clint Black *(1991)*
★ Alan Jackson *(1991)*
★ Vince Gill *(1991)*
★ Emmylou Harris *(1992)*
★ Marty Stuart *(1992)*
★ Travis Tritt *(1992)*
★ Charley Pride *(1993)*
★ Alison Krauss *(1993)*
★ Joe Diffie *(1993)*
★ Hal Ketchum *(1994)*
★ Bashful Brother Oswald *(1995)*
★ Martina McBride *(1995)*

1996 AND

COUNTING

Climbing the ladder to success, the Mavericks perform "Here Comes the Rain" before winning an award at the CMA show.

9

BOOM, BUST, OR WHAT?

What a year! In 1995 Garth Brooks surpassed Elvis in record sales; Alan Jackson surpassed Garth in awards; Reba McEntire surpassed Alan in concert attendance; and Shania Twain surpassed Reba in frequent-flyer miles flown to video sites. A number of country stars served as major pitch persons for a variety of products and services, from Fruit Of The Loom underwear to Visa credit cards, and a host of country stars graced movie-theater and television screens. Country music, with its increasing popularity throughout Europe and Australia and its recording sessions in Canada and China, became the shout heard 'round the world. And with duets once again coming from George Jones and Tammy Wynette, country music went back to the future.

The road continued for the Highwaymen—veterans Cash, Nelson, Jennings, and Kristofferson—and widened for such brilliant new acts as Alison Krauss and the Mavericks, igniting a retro-country movement that unites fans of all things traditional and all things cool. At year's end, an offbeat band named BR5-49 entered a studio to record an album for Arista Records. Before, during, and after BR5-49's discovery, this buzz band played into the wee hours night after night at Robert's Western Wear, a boot-and-beer honky-tonk wedged, physically and philosophically, between the Ryman Auditorium and the Wildhorse Saloon.

Despite the incredible crowd of talented singers over the past few years, country music still found room for such new acts as Wade Hayes, David Lee Murphy, and Terri Clark. With the plethora of bright new talents, something had to give; so, the competition level soared to an all-time high. Nobody knows who will survive, but everybody cares.

Awards were presented at the drop of a cowboy hat. The year's top winners were Alan Jackson, CMA's Entertainer of the Year; Reba McEntire, the ACM's Entertainer of the Year; Michelle Wright, the Canadian Country Music Association's Entertainer of the Year; Shania Twain, who won just about every other Canadian award except Male Vocalist; and Alison Krauss, who startled the country-music field by winning four CMA awards the first year she was nominated. The late Patsy

Cline received the National Academy of Recording Arts and Sciences (NARAS) Lifetime Achievement Award; Loretta Lynn, Patsy's friend, was honored with ACM's Pioneer Award; and the late and always great Roger Miller was elected to the hallowed halls of the Country Music Hall of Fame.

The Grand Ole Opry enjoyed another magnificent year, balancing old and new, traditional and contemporary, while serving as country music's umbilical cord to the past. Now seventy years young, the Opry's panorama of musical brilliance was reflected in the induction of its two newest members, twenty-nine-year-old Martina McBride and eighty-four-year-old Bashful Brother Oswald.

Festivals continued to enliven the landscape: Willie Nelson offered another of his July Fourth picnics—this one in Luckenbach, Texas, boosting that town's population from 3 to 15,000. Willie also staged the best Farm Aid yet, this one before 47,500 fans in Louisville, Kentucky, raising a million dollars for beleaguered family farmers. The Los Angeles–area Fanfest '95, in its second year, continued to grow, and Nashville's Fan Fair '95 once again brought fans and stars face-to-face for nearly a week's worth of activities. Cheyenne, Wyoming, saw Frontier Days, and the Phoenix area heard Country Thunder USA. Charlie Daniels and Hank Williams, Jr. performed at Denver's Rock the Rockies, and Murfreesboro, Tennessee, entertained some 40,000 fans, including Vice President Al Gore and his wife, Tipper, who came to see the 1995 Grand Ole Opry inductee Bashful Brother Oswald perform at Uncle Dave Macon Days. Alabama's June Jam drew thousands to their home-state home-brew extravaganza. In Morristown,

Ohio, nearly 95,000 turned out for Jamboree in the Hills '95. And near Cumberland, Maryland, stars especially liked the Rocky Gap Festival, where backstage amenities included massage, pinball, and fishing. The popularity of these star fests should continue to surge in 1996.

The year also proved to be a year of surprise. Early in the year, Alison Krauss was the name of a rather minor artist on a rather minor label, Rounder Records. By the end, in one of the most surprising developments, Alison and Rounder had spun to the top. Both deserve the new status. They have proven that big doesn't always mean better, that small doesn't always mean less.

Bard of the rednecks, Jeff Foxworthy scores with five charted albums and a new TV comedy show.

How about Garth Brooks not winning a single CMA award? That demonstrates the mercurial nature of the market. And what of a no-name group of grizzled vets from Tulsa, now named the Tractors, running off with the CMA Video of the Year Award? To paraphrase Alison Krauss as she accepted still another CMA award, "What in the world is going on here, folks?"

Ty Herndon latches on to another winner, Stephanie Bentley, who joined him on the hit "Heart Half Empty."

Comedian Jeff Foxworthy came out of nowhere with his redneck tales and ended the year with five country-chart albums, two on the pop charts, and a network TV sitcom.

And how about Ty Herndon, one of the best new talents to emerge from the explosion of new faces and new voices, who survived a summer scandal involving sex and drugs in Texas to surface, as he deserves, with an even stronger career and an even tighter grip on his life? Country radio stations should be praised for supporting Ty during his summer of discontent.

Wynonna, Mark Chesnutt, and Martina McBride entered the new year with brand-new babies. A daughter for Billy Dean and sons for Suzy Bogguss, John Berry, Marcus Hummon, Lee Greenwood, and Raul Malo continued the baby boom throughout the year.

Joining the ranks of the married were Ken Mellons, Jeff Cook of Alabama, Rosanne Cash, Jeff Huskins of Little Texas, Johnny Rodriguez (to a daughter of Willie Nelson), and Aaron Tippin.

On a sad note, the world of country music lost the Silver Fox, Charlie Rich; the Opry's Vic Willis; Kendall

Country music loses the golden-voiced Silver Fox, Charlie Rich, 62.

Hayes, who wrote *Billboard*'s number-one country song of all time, "Walk On By"; the singer Dick Curless; and Bill Boyd, the esteemed executive director of the Academy of Country Music.

Although cautious optimism remains the prevalent attitude in Music City, there's not an artist or an executive in this boom business who doesn't fret about a potential bust. It has happened before, they all recall, and it could happen again, they all fear. Like the countryside itself, and the hill country it hails from, country music has always been a portrait in peaks and valleys. They remember the euphoria of the early urban-cowboy days, when country music couldn't do wrong if it tried. That form of country was forgettable fad music whose popularity was notoriously, and thankfully, brief.

How can country continue its surge? Unfortunately, it can't count on the pop-music market, which has prodded it to heights that five years ago were only pipe dreams. Rap music and grunge rock have driven millions of music listeners into the country camp, where lyrics are often more meaningful, songs more soulful, and performers more approachable. Some of these listeners have been converted; others will stick with country only until they find an audio alternative to satisfy their tastes.

So, country music should be braced for the possibility of a drop in record sales, radio airplay, mass media coverage, and overall popularity in the next year or two. That's one reason why the music moguls of Nashville are trying to broaden the base of country music overseas; expanding an international market will soften the blow of any dips in the volatile domestic market.

Expect the domestic surge to wane while international acceptance grows. Expect the doomsayers of the national media to proclaim the death of country music, as they did fifteen years ago—and once again to have to swallow their wayward words. They never learn. They're mesmerized by the false gods of current acceptance, misguided by the new pulses in popularity, and beguiled by the loud noises of the new kids on the musical block. They wander astray because they don't understand the deep-rooted history of one of America's true original art forms. Fortunately, even with the worst-case scenario of a country-music slump, this resilient genre can be counted on to rise again, each time to a higher level than before.

How will country music conquer the future? High tech is not new to country music. Already the low-tech lyrics

From CD to CD-ROM: country stars join the computer revolution with the Country Vid Grid game.

have adapted to high-tech advances. Nashville studios helped lead the surge into digital technology, and Music City recording studios are the most advanced in the nation, thanks to sound pioneers such as Jimmy Bowen, a famed Nashville producer and former head of several major record labels, a man who refused to accept the low budgets and the low audio achievements of the earlier studios.

Classic country melodies will soon play out over classy computer systems. The first interactive CD-ROM product involving country musicians made its debut in 1995. The computer game Country Vid Grid allows players to view the music videos of Reba McEntire, Marty Stuart, Tracy Byrd, Vince Gill, Trisha Yearwood, Mark Chesnutt, and others.

How will country music conquer the future? By going back to the past. Do that Texas two-step. Do that shuffle move that Bob Wills and his Texas Playboys made magical a half-century ago. Go to your dance club, and dance your blues away. Most of all, play the classic country on the airwaves once again. Johnny Cash, Buck Owens, and Charley Pride—along with scores of still-great performers who helped make country music what it is today—are rarely heard on country radio, which is saturated with too many look-alikes, too many sound-alikes.

"People have eclectic tastes, but radio doesn't really reflect it," observed Emmylou Harris, whose 1995 album, *Wrecking Ball,* redefines country music. "If you go into their living rooms or wherever they keep their music, you won't find just one type of music. It seems odd there isn't a station where you can just hear all the great stuff. It used to be that way."

As usual, Willie Nelson put the situation in perspective when asked why radio plays mainly young acts. "I don't know, but I knew I was in trouble when I heard a guy the other day say 'I sure wish they'd play some of them old guys like Randy Travis and George Strait.' "

Let's enter a plea for country-music radio to program some of the great songs and the great singers of the past—the evergreen hits of Merle Haggard, Gene Watson, Gary Stewart, Don Williams, Vern Gosdin, George Jones. . . . In the frantic rush to get the latest hunkabilly onto the airwaves, radio programmers have pushed aside these veterans. It's an unfortunate, unfair, and vitiating development that the country-music industry—from the record companies to the radio stations—needs to address and correct.

How will country music conquer the future? By developing a coalition of cultures and styles that allows, for example, a Tejano-turned-country artist named Emilio to rocket up the charts with "It's Not the End of the World." By the creative cross-pollination of music, lifestyles, and culture that is typified by Michael Martin Murphey's grand and glorious WestFests, which merge cowboy and Native American, mountain man and country crooner, Tejano and western swing, classical and jazz, line dance and Indian dance, and cradle them lovingly in the Colorado Rockies in a golden time warp of past, present, and future.

How will country music conquer the future? By remaining geographically diverse, with powerful pockets of creativity located not only in Nashville but also in Texas, Canada, and California. And by remaining true to its heritage, which runs deeper than the roots of rock and rap and as deep as the well-entrenched roots of soul music, a not-so-distant cousin of country.

How will country music conquer the future? By going to Japan, Germany, and other untapped markets. Country went to Ireland in a big way in 1995, as it went to China, Latin America, and the Pacific Rim. The global village is still searching for new multicultural heroes in all forms of art and commerce. With uncomplicated, translatable

From Tejano to country, Emilio's fast-rising career reflects the title of his album Life Is Good.

lyrics, country music can easily transcend many borders and cultures.

Whether it's Kathy Mattea performing in Europe, Garth going Down Under, or Tracy Byrd playing in Alaska, country music has become the surround-sound of planet Earth. While Jerry Jeff Walker entertains a fun-loving, boot-scooting crowd in Luckenbach, Texas, and David Allan Coe spurs his audience to fever pitch with his always apropos "Take This Job and Shove It" (a number-one hit for Johnny Paycheck), radios will be tuning in to country music from America to Austria to Australia.

Perhaps that is the ultimate appeal. Country music is—and really always has been—part meaningful music, part soap opera, part human condition, part suspension of

With nearly 70 million weekly listeners, country radio ranks number one, up ahead of the Adult Contemporary and News/Talk formats. This year 2,346 stations programmed country music.

The Tractors achieved the fastest debut album to reach platinum status in country-music history—only three months after its release.

Country-music album sales revenues have more than doubled since 1990, reaching the $2 billion mark.

Reba McEntire is third on the all-time list of most gold albums by any female artist. Barbra Streisand has 31, Linda Ronstadt has 17, and Reba, 15. Dolly Parton follows close behind with 14.

TNN: The Nashville Network reaches nearly 60 million U.S. households and 5.4 million Canadian households.

CMT: Country Music Television reaches more than 31 million homes worldwide, including 1 million in Europe.

International record sales of country music exceed $215 million annually, most of which comes from Canada, England, Ireland, Switzerland, and Germany.

More than 400 radio stations outside North America program country music on a regular basis, reaching over 32 million listeners in 24 territories.

Total 1995 attendance for the Grand Ole Opry shows reaches the 650,000 mark.

belief, part pure pleasure. Even President Clinton has stated that country music "has greatly enriched our nation's cultural life. It is a vibrant part of our heritage— a celebration of the diversity, spontaneity, and energy that lie at the core of the American identity. For generations, Americans have enjoyed country music as a form of entertainment and a means of heartfelt expression." Hail to the Chief.

This year in country music has brought triumph, tragedy, birth, death, happiness, sadness, suspense, trauma, and trials. It has also brought America's most-beloved musical genre to a realm of higher acceptance and greater credibility. For all of these reasons, here's the catchphrase for 1996: Look out for 1997. And beyond.

Because, to paraphrase Alan Jackson . . .

The world's going country.
Look at them boots.
Going country.
Back to its roots.

Amen.